THE PRODUCERS:
CONTEMPORARY CURATORS IN CONVERSATION
(3)

Also available in the B.READ series:

B.READ / ONE
NEW SITES – NEW ART

Tuula Arkio, Jan Debbaut, David Elliott, Christian Jabornegg
Peter Jenkinson, András Pálffy, Dominic Williams

Edited by Sarah Martin and Sune Nordgren, 2000

B.READ / TWO
THE PRODUCERS:
CONTEMPORARY CURATORS IN CONVERSATION

James Lingwood & Sune Nordgren
Clive Phillpot & Matthew Higgs

Edited by Susan Hiller and Sarah Martin, 2000

B.READ / THREE
ARTISTS AT WORK

Daniel Birnbaum, Lynne Cooke, Kathryn Kanjo,
Friedrich Meschede, Richard Wentworth

Edited by Sarah Martin and Sune Nordgren, 2001

B.READ / FOUR
THE PRODUCERS:
CONTEMPORARY CURATORS IN CONVERSATION
(2)

Gilane Tawadros & Hans Ulrich Obrist
Frances Morris & Charles Esche
Guy Brett & Deanna Petherbridge

Edited by Susan Hiller and Sarah Martin, 2001

The Producers: Contemporary Curators in Conversation (3)

A series of public events, sponsored jointly by the Department of Fine Art, University of Newcastle and BALTIC, The Centre for Contemporary Art. The series is organised by Professor Susan Hiller, BALTIC Chair in Contemporary Art, and Vicki Lewis, BALTIC curator, and is held in the fine art lecture theatre at the University. Members of the public and the University are warmly invited to attend.

22 February 2001
Sharon Kivland and **Adam Szymczyk** in conversation
Chaired by Professor John Milner

8 March 2001
Ralph Rugoff and **Richard Grayson** in conversation
Chaired by Professor Susan Hiller

15 March 2001
Lisa Corrin and **Jon Bewley** in conversation
Chaired by Andy Thomson

Edited by Susan Hiller and Sarah Martin

First published in 2001 by BALTIC in collaboration with
the University of Newcastle, Department of Fine Art.

BALTIC
P.O. Box 158
Gateshead NE8 1FG
Great Britain
www.balticmill.com
ISBN 1-903655-05-6

University of Newcastle
Newcastle upon Tyne NE1 7RU
Great Britain
ISBN 0-70717-0127-7

Design by Ripe Design Consultancy, The New Inn, Bridge Street, Blaydon-on-Tyne.
Printed and bound in Great Britain by Cox and Wyman Ltd., Cardiff Road,
Reading, Berkshire.

Distributed by Cornerhouse Publications Ltd., 70 Oxford Street, Manchester M1 5NH.

ACKNOWLEDGMENTS

The publishing team and the organisers of this series would like to thank everyone who helped to make the events run smoothly, in particular Michael Brick, Lecturer in Painting at the University of Newcastle and Dave Pipkin, sound engineer. Special thanks also to Angela Horn, librarian in the Department of Fine Art, for her help with the transcripts.

This collection of curatorial conversations is the third publication documenting an ongoing series of events at the University of Newcastle. 'The Producers' series is organised jointly by the Department of Fine Art at the University and BALTIC, Gateshead. Since its inception in March 2000, it has contributed to expanding the context for contemporary art in the North East by bringing distinguished curators together to discuss their approaches to exhibition-making. Interest in these conversations to date has exceeded the original ambition of Andrew Burton (head of the Department of Fine Art), Vicki Lewis (BALTIC curator) and myself. We hope that by collecting the transcripts together, many more people will be able to enjoy what has been a memorable series of public debates.

SUSAN HILLER

The Producers: Contemporary Curators in Conversation (3)

CONTENTS

THE PRODUCERS: CONTEMPORARY CURATORS IN CONVERSATION

22 FEBRUARY 2001, UNIVERSITY OF NEWCASTLE, DEPARTMENT OF FINE ART

SHARON KIVLAND AND ADAM SZYMCZYK IN CONVERSATION
CHAIRED BY PROF. JOHN MILNER

VICKI LEWIS:

Hello and welcome. I'm Vicki Lewis, BALTIC curator, and tonight is the sixth in the series of curatorial discussions organised by BALTIC Professor of Contemporary Art, Susan Hiller, at the University of Newcastle. The theme of these events, which are jointly sponsored by the University and BALTIC, has been the changing role of the curator in contemporary artistic practice. Tonight's discussion will last around an hour and a half and we would like to invite everybody for a glass of wine afterwards upstairs in the lecture hall lobby. So without further ado, I would like to introduce this evening's distinguished participants.

Sharon Kivland is an artist, writer and curator who divides her time between the UK and France. She has shown widely over many years in Britain, Europe and North America. Recent projects include 'A Case of Hysteria', published in 1999 by Bookworks, London, and she is also one of eight artists taking part in 'Making History', a site-based project organised by Staffordshire University. She is currently working on a book that is an investigation of the psychic relations between the work of art and its viewer and, since 1997, has curated a series of seven exhibitions at the Centre for Freudian Analysis and Research.

Adam Szymczyk is a writer and curator. Since studying on the De Appel Curatorial Programme in Amsterdam in 1996 and subsequently returning to Poland, he has organised a number of diverse projects. In 1997 he co-founded the Foksal Gallery Foundation to support exhibitions, publications and research projects initiated by Foksal Gallery in Warsaw. For a time he published the magazine Material in addition to writing numerous texts on art for catalogues, magazines and newspapers. Since 1990 he has worked with a number of Polish and international artists for the Foksal Gallery and CCA Warsaw. Recent projects include the co-curation (with Charles Esche and Mark Kremer) of 'Amateur 1900 and 2000: Variable Research Initiatives' at the Kunstmuseum Gothenburg and currently, a project with artist Vija Celmins.

Last, but not least, Professor John Milner, who is the chair of today's discussion. John has produced a series of major publications on the history of art including 'Russian Revolutionary Art'; 'Vladimir Tatlin and the Russian Avant-Garde'; 'The Studios of Paris, Capital of Art in the Late Nineteenth Century' and 'Art, War and Revolution: France 1870-71'. Over to you, John.

JOHN MILNER:

It's a very great pleasure to welcome our two guests here this evening; it's a sign of the international determination of BALTIC, apart from anything else. BALTIC exists very thoroughly now, before the building opens, and it is quite an astonishing phenomenon. Seeing something like that emerge is quite different to meeting artist-curators who are working with the relationship between the roles of artist and curator as part of their own creative activity. So that, in a way, is what we're going to be looking at this evening. Sharon Kivland is going to speak first. Then Adam Szymczyk will speak and then we will have a debate. So, please don't feel shy about asking questions – difficult, demanding, easy – whatever they are, because they do concern a lot of people here in different ways. I'm going to say no more. Thank you very much – Sharon.

SHARON KIVLAND:

I will discuss seven shows that I made with the Centre for Freudian Analysis and Research (CFAR) in London, a Lacanian psychoanalytic training group, which for the first time had its own premises. The members' newsletter went out asking people to bring in pictures and one of the analysts and I said, 'This is going to be so awful, let's do an exhibition instead.' There's a visual arts working group that has taken up a proposal by Lacan – who frequently sketched out the meaning or goal of the work of art, always changing it – that the work of art occupies the place of the analyst. He proposes that it's the work of art that interprets the viewer: that, like the psychoanalytic encounter, there's something in the structure of viewer and artwork that brings the viewer to speech. It is not only works of art that might do this: for example, religion and magic might do it also. But it was the work of art that concerned us.

This (CFAR) is a place for the teaching and transmission of psychoanalysis. This is not an art gallery. The space has a different function and the exhibitions were part of it. Every Saturday there are seminars, some of which are open to the public. There have often been these objects, images, looking out from the walls at those who are captive, attentive or restlessly looking back or trying to avoid meeting the gaze of the object. The first show was called 'A Little Object' (1997), a silly title – as though we sought to make an image of something that can't have a form except as a void. It's a concept that is consistently present, throughout all of Lacan's teaching – the 'objet petit a' – a little object, lower case; a little other on which our desire is founded. Forty-five artists took part. Like all our subsequent exhibitions, it was accompanied by a discussion with invited speakers, for our aim was always one of an interdisciplinarity. We wanted to bring together people from different fields to question the nature and function of the work of art.

The idea of object a in the work of Lacan changes; from its status as 'a little other' which designates a reflexive, changeable relation with the ego, to a little object that can be separated from the body: the gaze, the voice, shit; something that comes away, to a hidden glory. The idea of agalma, which is in the love relation as well: the one who is loved has something that, if only they loved us back, we would have too. It's this idea of a transference that goes on with the work of art and with analysis but it's also that both are founded on a love relation. We don't have the object ourselves but we look for it in others who, like works of art, will continue to disappoint. It's certain that it's an object or the lack of an object that will cause anxiety, a real anguish. It's something that causes desire rather than fulfils it, and corresponds to both analyst and work of art.

The art object looks like it's something that should give meaning, but it doesn't. It's why we go to the title or why catalogue essays seem to get longer. The question most often invoked in relation to these exhibitions from an audience that was not a usual art audience was, 'Yes, but is it art?' It's a question that arises out of a real anxiety, indicating the questioner's sense that art should always be something other than it is.

(Slides) Colette Whiten showed a needlepoint work from a series. They're very small monochrome needle-points, deriving from pictures and photographs in the newspapers in which, for example, politicians are shaking hands, meticulously rendered. Underneath there's a darning mushroom as its support. In Seminar XI, Lacan talks about the object a as a bump that rises in cloth when you're darning it.

In 'Lexicon' (1997) we imagined that a text could become an image. In the forms of letters, words and the space between them, some meaning could be established. As meaning, it escapes too ready an interpretation, avoid-ing the mere substitution of one term for another. We were thinking of the works of art as ways of thinking about Lacanian theory, especially about interpretation. What does interpretation do? When it works it has an effect on the subject's unconscious but we don't know anything about the subject's unconscious; only the subject knows that.

This is the work of a Viennese artist, Sonja Gangl. This cute man with the 'R' on his chest is simply the support for the piece, which was given out at the opening as a tattoo. The letter 'R' was given out with a glass of wine and you could then transfer it onto your body and, being Lacanians, we were all going, 'Ah! It's the Real!' In fact, it did kind of erupt like the Real because the artist hadn't realised that she'd used some kind of glue that had a nasty effect on the skin, so afterwards everyone had skin eruptions of the letter 'R'. It was no longer a removable tattoo, it was actually inscribed on their bodies! (Audience laughter)

There was a psychoanalytic bookshop upstairs and the poet Thomas A. Clark made a series of works that were bookmarks inserted in books in the shop. They're little texts, beautiful things, which say things like, 'As if you were to turn away for a moment'. Rathbone Books would only let us put them in the Lacanian books – we weren't allowed to put them in Family Therapy! So there are always problems about our audience.

The works in 'Lexicon' seemed to demand some kind of interpretation whilst simultaneously behaving as if they supplied one. One of Stephane Le Mercier's three pieces is a bilingual translation of various European philosophers, the books cut in half and bound together. Tony Kemplen's piece again takes up the idea of demanding a reading, but at the level of an object – resisting reading. It's Plato's Symposium, which Tony Kemplen has run through a computer programme. He's taken out all the text, leaving only the punctuation. The book is transparent. It's the idea that meaning is only given when speaking stops, by punctuation.

In Seminar Two, Lacan warns of the dangers of trying to understand when one should simply listen. My collaborator, psychoanalyst Danuza Machado, has spoken about the lack of any intentionality in interpretation; that in psychoanalysis it's rare for something that might be considered to be a true interpretation to happen. In the course of a session the analyst might say, 'Ah yes, life is like that.' And the patient might come back and say, 'Ah yes, I understand what you say, life is like that.' It's not the usual sense of interpretation, but it disrupts meaning, and produces certain effects.

We wanted to imagine a moment of waiting, in which the work of art may be taken literally, 'à la lettre' and 'avant la lettre' as though we were entirely ignorant of theory. It is not that the works in this or any of the other exhibitions were invisible, rather that they can become so in the blink of an eye. Invisible in the sense that one doesn't have words for them or that one doesn't recognise them, or one has learnt too well to resist them. For they so clearly fail to be the sublime object in that they don't achieve occupation of the sacred place of the thing that will guarantee our jouissance. They are not unreadable, but neither can they be read like a book. They don't provide the comfort of reason, justice and polite intercourse.

The work of art is always an encounter with an impossibility, transgressing the possibility of any sort of satisfactory closure or completion of meaning, which reality appears to offer. This is what we addressed in the third exhibition, 'The Impossible' (1997). If representation is to play a role in the field of sense, it's as a veil covering the unrepresentable, but it's a cover up that's always incomplete, inconsistent. The veil itself is horrific in that it veils a horror, but because the horror is unrepresentable, the veil is much more frightening, for in drawing it back, one might see nothing at all. Luisa Bucciero installed a pink net curtain at the window. When approached, a light lights up behind it as you get very close, as though your own curiosity to see what's behind it actually displays your own desire to see it. What is concealed in the act of concealing is nothing. The form doesn't hide the content. It's useless to ask what a work means, but one might ask how it performs, what it performs. And how does it do so, this empty, inert object?

One may even cause the unthinkable to occur by a gesture. (Slide of work by Debbie Booth.) The piece is a slide in a little plastic slide projector. When you press it down, your act lights up a woman's face with a bruise on her cheek, under her eye, as though you've caused it. This is Martha Townsend's work, in which the soothing words of a child's lullaby, Rock-a-bye Baby, carry a far more terrifying message: a bowling ball is held in an immaculate leather strap. My assistant stood up too rapidly while installing this, and knocked himself out on the bowling ball!

The void may hold something because we fill it up with reveries; appearances produced by consciousness itself, because even reveries are better than emptiness. It's a loss that produces anxiety: it's not what we don't know, but what we do know that gives rise to anguish. If a gap is felt, it has to be filled with words, objects, images. Roberto Martinez saves all the chocolate wrappers accompanying the espresso at the end of a meal and writes the date and name of his companion beneath them. These encounters are never fulfilled at the level of desire, each little wrapper carrying the trace of the person who's been fiddling with it over his or her coffee, the mind clearly on something else. This is a work by Tonia Noikovitch; it's a plait escaping from the ceiling. Another work of Tonia's is a child's teddy bear, including his furry little genitals, an erection that rears up. It has this very nice effect: it sits on its shelf and people go up to it and go 'Ah! (gasp)'.

In the exhibition 'Disquieting Strangeness' (1998), Michelle Naismith's series of photographic drawings begin with a double image – a Siamese twinning where one girl's face merges into another, unable to separate without death. In the next, a girl cuddles a guinea pig having no doubt found a transitional object. In the last, a girl is carried off in an ambulance, wearing bunny ears. Stephen Cornell's set of photographs show a viewpoint from under a sofa, changing slightly each time, giving the rather unpleasant sense that something has scuttled across the floor. To see it you have to get a chair and take it over to a table and stand up at the table. A work by Cheryl Sourkes, a child's night light in which a child is falling through space. Another child bends to examine something in this piece by David Bate, and is overlooked by the reflective blank stare of a window. Models of Ernie, Elmo and the Cookie Monster moulded in Play-Doh, nailed onto the wall by Canadian artist Clair Cafaro, start out perfect, dry out, crack and deform. The child's plaything gathers a life of its own despite the organising principles of the mother.

One hardly notices Michelle Johnson's work at first: it oozes from the crevice of the wooden cage surrounding the staircase. Once noticed however, these little globules of whatever they are seem to proliferate and worse, seem to move towards you. From the apertures stuff emerges: nasty, organic-looking stuff recalling the most disgusting fluids of the body. The movement is, of course, that of the viewer's own body. The recognition of the oozing stuff is a recognition of that body, no longer held in check, subject to involuntary emissions accumulating in pools of spit, snot, ear wax and spilt drinks. If you think about vomit, one of the worst things about it is that it might move towards you. The body is not an adequate screen between things and our selves.

What is closest is the most alien, what is most homely can erupt most suddenly. A pot of jam, for example, now holding a preserved brain. The name of the former contents, 'Tiptree's Plum Conserve', altered to indicate that the jar now contains 'Blum Conserve', the name of the artist (Michael Blum). The object raises the question as to whether the artist is dead or alive, and one hardly likes to consider either. It hinges on a momentary doubt. This is a work by Jeremy Akerman: it's a photograph of his mother outside the house. The glass holds mother and son apart. In order to keep her in sight, to capture her image, he has to move with her. The inside and outside of the home are imperceptibly sliding into each other. A light flashed intermittently from the lavatory, disrupting attention while catching it. It's a work by Pavel Büchler. The familiar can trip you up, catch you out. It is the voice from behind you coming forth from one whom you did not expect to speak. The message is one of jubilation and anxiety and, as Mladen Dolar writes, 'at the juncture of elation and impending disaster'.

Francesca Gore's photograph shows a naked woman holding up her unconvincing guard dog, barring the door, but far more petrifying than the dog is the concealing cascade of her hair. Brushes are held in containers and turn into hair; hair rises up from a plughole or decorates a gown. Debbie Booth's cloak of furs is draped over the frame of a divan in the bookshop upstairs, a big window behind it, surrounded by analytic texts. In this collection, 'Ornament in the Field of Vision' (1998), hair turned to fur, feathers and pelts, as though a fetishist would build up his collection. We hold that the work of art is not a fetish object, because a fetish object is constructed to shore up against anxiety, which a work of art opens up.

This is the penultimate show, 'A Disturbance of Memory on the Acropolis' – a wonderful essay by Freud that reads more like an episode of Frasier. These are pictures of ballroom dancing trophies. The artist, Peter Willis, won't mind me telling you that when he was young his sister brought home a ballroom dancing trophy and was given an expensive gift by his parents. So he took up ballroom dancing and, in fact, became a champion. He would bring his trophies home to his father. Only years later he realised they meant little to his father. Yet he was offering them up – the son offering something up to the father. If you read Freud's essay you'll understand this story.

The last show was called 'There is no Sexual Relation' (1999). By now you've had a whirlwind tour of exhibitions you didn't see and you may feel rather like Freud on an Athenian hill. I'll give you a flick through. We argue that the missing part, the object little a, is the one thing that can't be represented in the analytic sense. This is why analysis may be likened to a work of art. In both domains desire is articulated with less than successful substitution; the missing object, the thing, is lacking anyway. Its lack gives rise to speech, talking about space it leaves. Like the beloved, it's only when this place or space appears to be occupied that one is moved, captured, spoken to. And

Lacan has a phrase: 'je te demande refuser ce que je t'offre parce que c'est pas ça'. ('I ask you to refuse what I offer you because that's not it'.) The object a takes the place of each missing partner as the object cause of one's desire. It's a staging and a masking that psychoanalysis and the work of art share as artifice. The fantasy enables one to sustain one's desire and to hold oneself at the level of one's vanishing desire. Object a makes its appearance in the void between subject and other.

Let me end with the story of the masked ball. A couple finally meet and the partners remove their masks only to discover their mistake. They met in Paris at the Opera Ball. When they removed their masks, sheer terror! It wasn't him! Her neither, by the way. It's the fantasy that provides the rationale for desire's deadlock and so it's not just the fantasy of successful sexual relation, but rather the fantasy of why it went wrong. Jouissance then must lie elsewhere; another time, another place, in the embrace of another. Fantasy constructs the scene of deprivation. It's why we don't get the work and someone or something must be to blame for our stupidity if we're not to suffer.

What all these exhibitions have been addressing is the proposition that the work of art occupies the place of the analyst. The work of art itself points to the impossibility of any relation between the viewer and the work. Like the sexual relation, the work can't complete the viewer; rather, it surprises the viewer as a subject of his or her own illusion and deception. At the end of the analytic relation, the analyst abandons the illusion that there is another supposed to know and is alone. 'I ask you to refuse what I offer you' is supplemented by a final 'that's not it'. I'll end with some words of Freud – 'Love for oneself knows only one barrier, love for others, love for objects' – and a reminder that while the work of art may share something with the place of the analyst, going to art galleries and museums won't cure you.

(Audience applause)

ADAM SZYMCZYK:

Thank you very much for inviting me here. The gallery I am involved with (Foksal Gallery) has existed in Warsaw since 1966. It's quite a unique situation because it is still in the same place it was in over thirty years ago and is still run by one of its founders, Wieslaw Borowski. Then there is a team of four younger curators: Malgorzata Jurkiewicz, Joanna Mytkowska, Andrzej Przywara and myself.

So as I said, the gallery was founded in 1966 and was, and still is, a public space. It was a former library of books on Karl Marx, Friedrich Engels and Vladimir Ilych Lenin. For political reasons, towards the end of the sixties, these books became quite irrelevant in Poland so they – 'they' meaning the authorities – liquidated this library: they removed the books, which made this space available. There was a group of artists and art critics who were meeting in a café nearby who already had an experience of running a gallery in the late fifties/early sixties, and they started talking about the new space. Then came the artist Henryk Stażewski, who said, 'Why don't you start a gallery here? It's a very nice palace.' So they wrote a letter to the proper authorities, who agreed to let the space for artistic experimentation. So all this avant-garde rhetoric was actually used to persuade the people in charge that it was worth taking a risk with a group of young artists who wanted to make some experiments there.

There was an organisation called PSP, which had huge workshops where artists made decorations for all sorts of official celebrations, of which there were plenty in the Communist era. It was quite handy because the gallery was part of the administration of these workshops, so the artists who made works in the gallery could use the workshops that were otherwise used for official festivities. Then the structures changed several times, but the position of the gallery was secondary or inferior to the bigger structure that remained. And it's still like that, ten years after the end of Communism. It's strange that the situation has remained the same, in a way.

The gallery occupies the ground floor of a wing of a neo-Renaissance palace in the centre of Warsaw. There is an exhibition room of thirty-five square metres and two small offices. It's a perfect white box with the opportunity to open four windows: two to the garden and two facing the inner courtyard of this palace.

I'll show you slides from some exhibitions that took place there in the late sixties, at the starting point of the gallery, and also in the early seventies, which for us was the most productive and interesting time in the gallery's history. Then I'm going to show you some projects that I have been involved with over the past couple of years; in other words, the present activity of the gallery.

(Slides) This exhibition from 1967, just a year after the gallery opened, was the first show of Henryk Stażewski. In 1966 Stażewski was sixty-eight years old and he was among the first generation of Polish avant-garde artists before the Second World War. In 1927 he invited the Russian Constructivist artist Kazimir Malevich to have an exhibition in Warsaw which was held at the Hotel Polonia and it was actually the first show of Malevich outside Russia. I'm telling you about these two exhibitions to point out the fact that in 1966 Stażewski represented the continuity of the avant-garde tradition. But it was not as simple as that. The next slide shows how the revolutionary consciousness of the first avant-garde translates into the revolution of 1968. It is actually Stażewski (in the photograph) who is smoking a pipe, and he's talking to one of the hippie guys from Warsaw at that time. There were not many of them in Warsaw in the late sixties, but there were still some small groups of people who were just meeting, talking and making music. Stażewski was always interested in talking to these people because for him they represented the upcoming revolution.

This is the early exhibition (1966) by Wlodzimierz Borowski who was also part of this initial group of six or seven artists and art critics who started the gallery. It was called a 'Syncretic show' and the artist is sitting in a box which is constructed inside the exhibition space surrounded by lots of tiny mirrors that are hung on strings, and the room is half-dark, half-light. The audience cannot enter the room, they can only stand in the entrance – there are two small entrances, one on the left, one on the right. They can see him (Borowski) and he can see them in these mirrors, but the audience can never get a complete image of what is actually in the space. And to make it even more obvious or apparent, there are these constructions built of plastic flowerpots with needles stuck into them, to prevent the viewers from entering the space in a very literal way.

An early piece (1964) by Edward Krasiński, who was also among the six people who started the gallery. It's called 'The Spear' and is a sculpture that is supposed to hang in the air in the landscape. So it's hanging on this very thin string and the idea behind the piece is to make the impossible possible: to free the sculpture from the support. This is the exhibition (1966) of linear sculptures made of cables and wires by Edward Krasiński. The space is lit up and this is a good example of what they would call an 'environment' – rather than an installation – which implies thinking about the site where it all takes place as something very crucial for experiencing the work. So it was like a total space of form and lights.

Another exhibition of Krasiński from 1968, which again are these linear sculptures and other works made of metal tubes, plastic cables, pieces of string and other similar, quite insubstantial materials. What is important here is the presence of these pedestals which are blocking the access to pieces and that make you feel quite uncomfortable while walking between them. In 1992 we had an exhibition of an Austrian artist, Franz West, which was called 'Investigations of American Art', and he actually used a similar trick. He showed quite typical pedestals for sculptures and on them there were small, blobby pieces made out of papier-maché, gauze, plastic and polyester. At that point we started thinking that maybe there is a deeper relationship between what we were busy with in the nineties and the exhibitions from the late sixties. We started to research the archives, which resulted in a series of publications that are trying to make a link between our current activity and the work of the people who founded the gallery. So this is just to say that that period is very important for us in our current practice as curators in this space.

This is a slide of our office; it looks like that now. It hasn't changed much – we have the same kind of furniture – and so it's very strange, a bit like time travel, when you enter the gallery. Right from the very beginning, the gallery was involved in various kinds of activities apart from exhibitions, both inside and outside the gallery. This is a performance during a symposium of art critics in the town of Zielona Góra in Poland (1969) by a group of artists that called themselves the Second Group, although there was no First Group preceding them! They are just setting up a small workshop with banners saying, 'We are able to make copies of contemporary artworks at your request. So you are welcome to bring us your favourite artwork and we'll make a copy for you and then you can walk away with a pretty cheap copy of your favourite artwork.'

This is a performance – I'd prefer to call it a 'situation' – under the title 'A Four Person Hat' (1969). It's people who were working at the gallery wearing this huge box as a sort of hat. They're moving along the pavement in the city and they cannot, apparently, see outside. I think perhaps for them it represented the fact that this gallery was in the strange situation of being a 'white box', isolated from the political and social context. They simply tried to show that they were closed to any sort of influence from outside and they wanted to fight this state of things.

This is one of the very early Happenings by Tadeusz Kantor, a famous Polish playwright. Kantor travelled to the U.S. in the late fifties and I think he was familiar with the Happenings of Allan Kaprow. He came to Poland and staged a number of these performances or Happenings as he called them. This one, from 1967, included a team of postmen from the local post office who were carrying a huge letter addressed to the Foksal Gallery. While the postmen were walking and carrying the letter, there were speakers who would report to the gallery via a walkie-talkie saying, 'They're coming,' or 'They're just round the corner.' So the tension in the gallery audience slowly built and then the letter was brought to the gallery and destroyed in an apparently spontaneous, frenetic outburst of violence.

Another Happening by Kantor, also from 1967, called 'The Panoramic Sea Happening' and you see Kantor directing his actors or the audience. His Happenings were very carefully choreographed and designed and he was always in full control of what was going on. The Happening consisted of several parts that were like little mise-en-scène or tableaux vivants, living images. This is a re-enactment of the famous painting by Gericault, 'The Raft of the Medusa'. This is another part where Edward Krasiński, the artist whose works I showed you earlier, is conducting a sort of sea concerto, with the audience sitting on the shore. And he's there wearing a quite impeccable tuxedo, just conducting the waves.

This slide shows part of an installation by Zygmunt Targowski (1971) who was also a photographer of the gallery. He did most of the photographic documentation in this early period but he was also making his own work which was quite atypical in Poland at that time, because he was not interested in 'arty' subjects, but more in the everyday and vernacular. He mainly took photographs of construction sites in Warsaw and the surrounding area, starting with photographs of houses that were about to be demolished to make room for new buildings. He also photographed the first apartment blocks under construction. He had a huge archive of these photographs that consisted of perhaps five thousand images and then in 1969, he died in a motorbike crash which was just before he completed what he intended to show at the gallery. Since he left a very precise outline of how the photographs should be installed – all over the walls, on the floor and on the ceiling of the gallery, composed in a grid with no empty space between them – the exhibition was realised a year after his death.

Krzysztof Wodiczko (1973), an artist of whom you may have heard and who became famous later on for his projections on public buildings in the U.S, Europe and elsewhere. This is an early work called 'Vehicle'. In this piece the movement of a person walking backwards and forwards on the top of the vehicle is converted into the forward movement of the vehicle. The speed of the vehicle is half the walking speed of the person and it doesn't matter in which direction the person on the vehicle is walking because it can only move in one direction. The piece was designed to be used exclusively by the artist and was a kind of metaphor for the situation of artists and intellectuals in Poland at that time. It meant, very straightforwardly, that no matter which way you walk and how long you think, the whole thing is moving steadily in one direction. At that time in Poland if you said, as an artist, that you would like to make an experimental vehicle to test in the city, you would probably be given the permission to do so. So in a way, making art was an excuse of a sort. You could not make a direct political statement because then you would just be put in jail. But you could at least make artworks that covered something of what you were thinking and talking about with your friends.

Apart from the exhibitions, another interesting element of the activity of the Foksal Gallery in the late sixties/early seventies, were a number of projects that went beyond the concept of the exhibition in the gallery. They were actually planned as events with the potential to start in the gallery and then spread out into the city. This is from the exhibition called 'Winter Assemblage' (1969), where the artists were asked to take the gallery as a point of departure for activities that would then spread out or disappear into the city, with the gallery potentially being left empty.

This is Zbigniew Warpechowski, one of the artists who was in that show. He first built a small corner within the gallery space and then he quickly made a drawing around himself, sitting in the corner, so that when he finished the drawing and stood up, he left behind him a drawing of lines surrounding an empty centre. Basically, he constituted the work only by leaving it.

This is a project with Polish artist Pawel Althamer, that we did at the beginning of last year in Warsaw, called 'Brodno 2000'.[1] Brodno, where Pawel lives, is a quite uninteresting area with huge apartment blocks. What you see here is the final part of a process that took three months to complete. The last half-hour, when the lights were finally turned on, was not as important as the process of negotiating with the inhabitants of this block and persuading them, in different ways, to participate. Althamer succeeded to a point – some of the inhabitants, who didn't want to participate, protested. But generally it was extremely successful, and as you see, it looks a little bit like a drive-in cinema, with all these cars belonging to people from the area parked there. The audience for the event was not the 'art people', who were a tiny minority, but those who lived nearby. Another thing that was important was that once it became known within the local community that such a thing was going to take place, all kinds of organisations tried to take it over. So the priest in

[1] In which the inhabitants of a Warsaw apartment block produced an illuminated '2000' on the façade of the building using the light from their windows. See also B.Read / Four, p.75.

the church would say in a sermon that the light that you're going to switch on – or not going to switch on – on that day in your windows, is in fact a divine light and you should remember that! (Audience laughter) So there were various ways to use this event, which in itself was quite innocent, for different ends. And it's important to mention that it was not organised for January 1st or anything like that; it was not meant to celebrate the year 2000. Rather, it was a belated celebration, which took place on February 27th. The reason Althamer chose '2000' instead of, for instance, saying 'Hello' or something like that, is because 2000 seemed to be a kind of idea that people would share, no matter what their ideology: we are living in the year 2000, so let's say so.

This is a project that took six months and started last year ('Creeping Revolution' 1999). We invited five artists to make works in the gallery and we told them that the work needed to be made either on the floor, on the ceiling or on the wall, but it had to be two dimensional. No hanging anything in the space and no setting up sculptures in the space; the work had to stay flat. Jim Lambie did the floor and Richard Wright made a painting in a corner. Then in the entrance you had walls painted by Andrzej Szewczyk with normal household paint: the pattern was made with a hand roll, which is still used for decorating private apartments in the south of Poland. There is a blue stripe of Scotch tape by Edward Krasiński running around the interiors and two almost invisible paintings of surfing boards made with white paint on the white wall by Jaroslaw Flicinski. It was important that the exhibition continued, so after two months we invited the German artist Peter Pommerer to come up with another work. We wanted to continue this exhibition up to the point where the whole gallery was totally full and you could not possibly put any more artworks inside. Also, because this exhibition lasted quite a long time – six months – it gave us an excuse to concentrate on other projects outside the gallery, of which 'Brodno 2000' was one. So it was possible for us to co-ordinate quite a complicated project with our team of only three people because we did not have to work on exhibition after exhibition in the gallery space. In a way, it was far more interesting than just changing exhibitions every month, as we usually do.

This is the last work I would like to show you, which was also made within the framework of the 'Creeping Revolution' project, by Piotr Uklanski (1999), a Polish artist living in New York. You may know him from the piece he showed at the Photographers' Gallery in London a couple of years ago, called 'The Nazis'. In Warsaw, he first collected damaged pottery or tableware of all kinds from different factories and then we brought around twenty huge boxes of this stuff into the gallery while this exhibition with Jim Lambie and Richard Wright was still on. We had to sort it very carefully and then a mosaic was made outside the gallery, on the three walls of a huge pillar containing the staircase of a department store called 'Smyk' in the centre of Warsaw: a very fine modernist building from the late fifties which has been left quite intact until now. The mosaic itself alluded to similar works that were made in Poland through the seventies and eight-ies as public commissions. Famous artists in Poland were asked to make mosaics for public buildings and usually these mosaics represented some kind of allegorical or mythological subject. Uklanski's abstract mosaic was very ugly and at the same time, strangely beautiful. Most people hated it because it reminded them of something quite unpleasant from twenty years ago.

This is a still from 'Feature Film' by Douglas Gordon, with whom we did an exhibition two years ago. The show had this very lengthy title which was, 'Virtually every film and video work that I did since 1992, presented on monitors, some silent, some with headphones and all running simultaneously'. As I told you, the space is thirty-five square metres and Gordon's ambition was to present all his video pieces from the last couple of years. We ended up setting up thirty-five monitors, so after ten minutes the temperature in the room was very high! However, we screened Gordon's 'Feature Film' in a far more relaxing situation, in the cinema in Warsaw. That's just another type of our activity – trying to find partners in the city with whom we can collaborate on various projects. Finito, thank you.

(Audience applause)

JOHN MILNER:

Thank you very much to both our speakers. There's a great deal there that you might want to pick up on. So, let's start with a question from the floor.

QUESTION:

Sharon, you commented at some point, and I can't quite remember how you put this, that work didn't have any meaning and so it was interpreted in catalogues and this was why there was much more commentary on work these days. And then Adam showed us an interesting piece called 'Vehicle', where the meaning, in a sense, couldn't be articulated because of the oppressive political climate of the time, but clearly the meaning was embedded in the work. I wondered if you had any thoughts about that?

SHARON KIVLAND:

I think that the meaning is embedded in the work at a particular time. It has particular cultural significance at the time, but that's also then determined afterwards. I think someone seeing the work at the time might say, 'I know what this means,' because it's repeating their own experience. This is the sense, I think, in which the work of art shows the effect of ideology upon the subject and says what can't be spoken, or it demonstrates it or acts it out in some way. But I think, made ten, twenty years later, its meaning shifts – or one endeavours to recuperate its meaning, but it's different.

JOHN MILNER:

Does that apply to your exhibitions, too?

SHARON KIVLAND:

Yes.

JOHN MILNER:

So is the documenting of them a form of continuous conversation? You both referred to the history of your projects and in a way, you were producing a kind of archive of slides and commenting upon them. Do you think there are significant shifts and changes?

SHARON KIVLAND:

Yes. There seems, at the moment, to be an opening up of interest in history that's been forgotten. We haven't had any history in art for ten years, except art history, but there seems to be a return to works that have gone under-ground, that young artists are now able to talk about and to bring into their own discourse. And I don't think that happened for quite a long time.

JOHN MILNER:

You were very aware of the history of your gallery, Adam: Stażewski and the sixties and so on. You spoke as if you had an ongoing dialogue with the past.

ADAM SZYMCZYK:

In the story about Stażewski I was just trying to speak figuratively about certain links, but the issue of history has been at the core of this gallery since it was founded. For instance, these wooden boxes (in Foksal Gallery's office) were designed by the same artist who did 'Vehicle' and contained the documentation from the sixties and seventies and also, to an extent, from the eighties. But suddenly it turned out, in the late nineties, that although we have lots of boxes that are still empty and that can be filled with documentation, this documentation keeps growing and expanding. It seems that you need many more letters and faxes to make an exhibition nowadays than you needed thirty years ago. And I can say that because all these documents from the early period are quite beautifully stored and you can see that, for instance, Lawrence Weiner was doing a show at the gallery with just three letters! (Audience laughter) It's kind of exceptional because nowadays, no matter who you work with, you receive say, twenty faxes before you actually get going. It's a bit scary, but it's also very interesting, so we keep this historical archive as a kind of monument. It's slightly ironic because the theoretical activity of this gallery, from the early seventies onwards, was very much against the idea of self-preservation and documentation and turning this space into an inert historical site. Nevertheless, it ended up having this monumental archive of photographs and letters.

JOHN MILNER:

Is that something that you have, that your slides show, Sharon? Were they your personal archive? After all, you weren't working in a gallery as such?

SHARON KIVLAND:

No. The slides are in a folder. I dupe some of them and then I give them to the artist, but then I don't have the originals because I find out I've duped the wrong ones! I know that in ten years time I won't have anything that approaches an archive.

JOHN MILNER:

Perhaps you were going to say something about the ephemeral nature of exhibitions, in that case?

SHARON KIVLAND:

I don't have to preserve its history because it's not a museum or a gallery practice. It comes from a particular way of working: CFAR only exists because of its members and its members change. So it's continually changing – it's not even an institution, because as analysts you have to undo the institutional nature of analysis or you lose what analysis might be. But, I have to say, because I'm also an artist and have to be aware of slides and sending out history, we did do a book which is an issue of our Journal[1] and that's going to be the history when the slides have gone. Don't know who'll find it, where they'll find it or how they'll find it or think what it is, because it'll be reinterpreted or interpreted quite differently from our intention. But being aware of that, when Marc du Ry and I edited it, we did not put in installation shots. We asked every artist who participated to remake their work for the format of the book. Some people did that in extremely inventive ways and other people sent an image of the piece taken by a real photographer in a proper photographic studio, so it looked fantastic. Then other people really took on this new vehicle which clearly was more interesting for my co-editor and myself.

[1] 'In the Place of an Object', Journal of the Centre for Freudian Analysis and Research, Special Issue 2000, Editors Sharon Kivland and Marc du Ry, Aldgate Press, London, 2000.

JOHN MILNER (TO SUNE NORDGREN):

Sune, do you have feelings about this? Have you been documenting every bucket of concrete that goes into the BALTIC?

SUNE NORDGREN:

Of course! Adam talked about the sixties and seventies – it's very, very important to be able to go back and look at what's been done before. In terms of Foksal, it's been the kind of 'eye of the storm', the focus point for new contemporary art in Poland for thirty, forty years. I mean, all of the Polish artists that we see today, Miroslaw Balka, Leon Tarasewicz, everyone we see around now, started at the Foksal, so of course it's important. It's ironic that it is so complicated to do an exhibition today. You can't, even as the director of a museum, go directly to the artist and ask him or her for an exhibition. You have to go through galleries and agents and lots of other things before you can reach the artist. So there is this growing infrastructure around the artist – and it's pretty scary, I agree, but I don't know what to do about it.

SHARON KIVLAND:

But that's more particularly the case if you want to do a show as a gallery or museum. There are other ways of making exhibitions, where you don't have any of that: spaces like CFAR, where all the discussion is directly with the artist, probably over a drink at another opening, where we would say, 'We have an idea. Are you interested?' And they say yes or no.

JOHN MILNER:

I'm sure Sune does that!

SHARON KIVLAND (TO SUNE NORDGREN):

So you're presenting quite an institutional line on it.

SUNE NORDGREN:

Of course it starts in a café; every exhibition, I suppose, does that. But in order to make the exhibition happen, that's what I mean. Of course, it's a different thing if you're in a so-called institution, because you have to answer to the public, you have to answer to people who've invested money and all sorts of other things. It is different of course, depending on the spaces you're responsible for. It's difficult to compare the Tate with Foksal, for example, and I wouldn't say that one is more important than the other. I don't think so, to be honest, but they are different.

JOHN MILNER:

But Sharon, could you say something about your public, your audience? How could people become aware of the activities of this group (CFAR) in the place that was not a gallery and wasn't signalling its work?

SHARON KIVLAND:

We do an art mailing and we do an analytic mailing and if we have any extra money, we will take an ad in an art magazine which, on the whole, doesn't seem worth it, very small audience. It's not aimed at a big audience. In the end it functions within the group Lacan.

JOHN MILNER:

Do your audience ever become a part of the group? Do you encourage involvement in the debates? You say some of the debates are public.

SHARON KIVLAND:

Yes. It's one of the reasons the project stopped, because I felt it was enough and someone else needed to do it. So now there are a couple of cartels which are work groups within Lacanian analysis who are working on things, but they haven't done exhibitions before and we prefer to have something in the space. We're putting things on there but it's with a rather different feeling: the product isn't quite the same.

JOHN MILNER:

How would these people find out what you're doing? How would the people in the audience here who have seen all this interesting material, find out where the next event is?

SHARON KIVLAND:

They would contact our administrator who would send them information about it. But it would be the same way you would find out how to become a Lacanian analyst!

JOHN MILNER:

It may not have occurred to everyone here!

SHARON KIVLAND:

It's very particular, and not everyone would be interested.

COMMENT FROM AUDIENCE:

I was just thinking about the difference between the work that's shown at these two galleries. (To Sharon Kivland) If you're talking about works being unspeakable, perhaps it's because of the work you're putting in your gallery, but if nobody can see it…

COMMENT FROM AUDIENCE:

I think you're talking about the relationship that the viewer has with the piece of art, and obviously you can't speak about something which is a very intimate kind of thing. But there is a certain relationship which you can have, such as the 'Brodno 2000' piece, which brings in this wider audience.

JOHN MILNER:

Do you share those views, Adam?

ADAM SZYMCZYK:

There's always the danger of the event becoming merely spectacular and, of course, on many levels the work is always recuperated. Whatever live event you may participate in, it ends up as a slide. 'Brodno 2000' was a very experiential piece on one hand, because the people were there and they were just having fun, they were making comments and so on. The art is not about this or that slide.

COMMENT FROM AUDIENCE:

No, exactly. But I think that the idea that anybody could have seen it – that in itself is more interesting.

ADAM SZYMCZYK:

Also, a funny thing was, the way the work was received was then carried on by tabloid magazines: the next day you'd have an image on the front page of a bad magazine or daily newspaper in Warsaw. On the very first day it was not subject to art criticism; they basically spoke about it as an event of some kind and this was pretty much the intention of the artist, to have it fully dissolved into the social, including the way it's received and understood. So it didn't demand a more complex reading first hand but of course later on, journalists had to write something. For us it was important that we went out of the gallery so we did not have to invite the 'vernissage' audience to come round and see the work. Rather, it was something that took place outside and was very open. It was not ours, in a way; it didn't belong to anybody. That was quite good.

JOHN MILNER:

That reminds me of Tristan Tzara talking about art as a virgin microbe. (To Adam Szymczyk) But your gallery is well known. It has a kind of image and history and people and it's in the centre of the city of Warsaw, so people would expect it to have some kind of public profile. (To Sharon Kivland) That is quite different to your situation, where you have a collective thinking about Lacanian psychological theory.

SHARON KIVLAND:

Which is a kind of theoretical proposition we want to examine within a small group of people.

JOHN MILNER:

So they're quite different. (To audience) Do people have views about working collectively? Any gallery works collectively to some extent...

COMMENT FROM AUDIENCE:

I think if the artists are working collectively it helps the viewer – they feed off each other. You can get more out of the works when you see others, whereas quite often the works are so disparate and you're all over the place trying to make connections.

QUESTION (TO ADAM SZYMCZYK):

The gallery has occupied the same space for over thirty years and you obviously have some problems – like overheating! – but you haven't expanded. You're not in the business of expanding except in reaching out into the city space. Is it a question of resources or is it a conscious decision to keep that historical space?

ADAM SZYMCZYK:

It's partly a decision to work in the space because it's historically loaded and therefore interesting and it can be researched and so on. Secondly it's a public space which is currently administered by the local government of the Masovian Voivodship – which is the region of Warsaw and its surroundings. Four years ago we started the Foksal Gallery Foundation because we were highly underfunded. We didn't have any capital in the beginning, so the Foundation is a tool for bringing in money for the projects that we're trying to realise. The fact that we have a Foundation allows us to be more flexible in terms of facilitating the work of artists and also being independent to an extent, independent from this funding from the city or the region, which is highly insufficient. Recently it also became very difficult for political reasons, because the whole bureaucratic structure which is above us changed to a new kind of structure with very similar problems. It may all end up in us either being fired or sent home, in which case we can probably operate in a different location still keeping the name of the Foksal Gallery Foundation or perhaps doing something else. In the last four years we tried hard to get rid of the necessity of working as the Foksal Gallery. So now we are prepared to operate in very different circumstances if necessary. But for now it's just convenient and it's worth it to try to work from within this space – it's like a given.

QUESTION (TO SHARON KIVLAND):

You were talking about the Lacanian thing where you have to circle the object, but if you've got books, can you not just read the book and enjoy the art from the book? If you're going to document exhibitions in the book and the book is going to be some kind of history, can you experience the artwork from the book instead of in the gallery?

SHARON KIVLAND:

You haven't experienced. The book is mostly the texts or versions of the discussions that accompanied each show and then there are artists' pages, which endeavour to give some other kind of experience of what one might have seen had one been there. So already the images in the book come in place of an object, but are not the object.

QUESTION:

So you do need the object as well?

SHARON KIVLAND:

No.

QUESTION:

So books could theoretically take over?

SHARON KIVLAND:

No. They would be a different experience. It's two different modes of experience; it's not one or the other.

JOHN MILNER:

Well, it just remains for me to thank both of our speakers.
That was very stimulating and I'm sure you can pick up
some of these points in a few minutes over a drink outside
and I'd encourage you to do that.

(Audience applause)

THE PRODUCERS:
CONTEMPORARY CURATORS IN
CONVERSATION

8 MARCH 2001, UNIVERSITY OF NEWCASTLE,
DEPARTMENT OF FINE ART

RALPH RUGOFF AND RICHARD GRAYSON
IN CONVERSATION
CHAIRED BY SUSAN HILLER

VICKI LEWIS:

Hello and welcome everyone. I'm Vicki Lewis, BALTIC
curator, and today is the seventh in the series of discus-
sions between distinguished curators, organised by
BALTIC Professor of Contemporary Art, Susan Hiller.
These events are jointly sponsored by the Fine Art
Department at the University of Newcastle and the
BALTIC and their theme is the many and varied

approaches to the role of the curator in initiating, commissioning and presenting contemporary art.

It gives me great pleasure to introduce the speakers for today's discussion. Richard Grayson is currently the director of the Sydney Biennale 2002. An artist, writer and curator who divides his time between the UK and Australia, he was a founding member of The Basement Group (Newcastle-upon-Tyne, 1979-84) and director of the Experimental Art Foundation (Adelaide, Australia, 1991-98). Recent exhibitions of his art include the solo exhibitions 'Negative Space' (Yuill Crowley Gallery, Sydney, 1999), 'ahistoryofreading' (Kewlona Art Gallery, Canada, 1999) and the group exhibition 'Sporting Life' (Museum of Contemporary Art, Sydney, 2000). He has written widely, both as a reviewer and for artists' catalogues.

Ralph Rugoff is a writer and curator. After several years in London he has returned to America where he recently became director of the CCAC Institute in San Francisco and Oakland, California. He has been a regular contributor to Frieze, Artforum, LA Weekly and the Financial Times. 'Circus Americanus' (Verso, 1995) is a collection of some of these essays. He is also co-author of the book 'Paul McCarthy'. In addition to his writing, he is noted for such curatorial excursions as 1997's 'Scene of the Crime' (UCLA Armand Hammer Museum, Los Angeles), 'At the Threshold of the Visible: Miniscule and Small Scale Art, 1964 – 1996' (New York Independent Curators), and with Lisa Corrin, last year's 'The Greenhouse Effect' (Serpentine Gallery, London, 2000).

Last but not least, BALTIC Professor Susan Hiller, who is the chair of tonight's discussion and who should need no further introduction.

SUSAN HILLER:

Thanks very much Vicki. Welcome to all of you. I'm certainly looking forward to hearing what today's speakers have to tell us. The usual way that we do this is that each of the invited guests gives a relatively brief presentation dealing with their own approach to curating exhibitions, then we have a very informal discussion followed by some wine. Ralph will begin.

RALPH RUGOFF:

I'll just tell you about a few exhibitions that I've curated to give you some idea of my background. I started out as a writer writing about art. Unfortunately, I have a low boredom threshold, so I often got bored looking at exhibitions, even exhibitions where I liked some of the work, and wondered why that was so. I started thinking that maybe there was more to an exhibition than just the work that was in it and that's when I started thinking about curating. Because there are very subtle things that can happen in an exhibition that can actually prevent the work from doing its job, which as far as I am concerned, is basically to unsettle you in one way or another: I think that's what all interesting art does. It can unsettle you visually, perceptually, conceptually, whatever; even something just purely beautiful is unsettling.

Just by coincidence, at the same time (1989), I was giving a lecture at an art college in California on 'patheticism', which is a term I came up with to refer to a body of literature whose protagonists were rather sad-sack bachelor characters and completely incompetent in their everyday lives. I was very interested in the response this kind of writing provoked in me because these people were incredibly sad, but most of the time I was laughing hysterically reading this stuff. So I gave this lecture and Mike Kelley was on the faculty of the school and came up to me after the talk and said, 'You've got to curate a show based on this idea. I'll help you. We'll do it at my gallery, we'll pay for it, etc.' So I said, 'Great, OK!' I'd never thought of curating before, but there were works of art that I was seeing when I was thinking of this. This was a subject that was very close to my own heart, for various reasons that I need not go into but you can only guess at! So I got into doing this exhibition. I don't have any slides, which is rather pathetic of me, but I'll describe some of the things that were in the show. You may know some of this work.

There was, for instance, a wonderful sculpture by Georg Herold made from a used and stitched-together piece of underwear that was inverted on a small scaffold, so it looked a bit like a Noguchi lamp or a very soiled version of an Alp. The title actually referred to one of the Austrian Alps and this looked like the kind of thing you could probably go home tonight and make. One of the things about the pathetic that interested me was that it aspired to be something great, but failed. And this work aspired to conjure up a snowy mountaintop, a great peak, and you could kind of see that, but it also didn't fully work. With this show, 'Just Pathetic' (American Fine Arts Co., New York, 1990), I was really interested in works of art that didn't talk about failure, ineptitude, incompetence or impotence, but actually embodied these qualities. This was in response to a lot of artwork in the 1980s where the artist seemed to be speaking from a position outside the culture and addressing the viewer and saying, 'You're manipulated by the mass media, you're manipulated by advertising, you're manipulated by this ideology or that ideology.' It seemed to me fairly obvious that we were all completely vulnerable to mass media as a purveyor of one ideology or another. I could go and see any movie...I could go and see ET and cry! There was no way you could really be outside of this. So I was interested in artwork that, rather than wagging its finger at you, actually seemed to embody the effects of living in this kind of situation. This work did, in one way or another.

Another piece in the show was by an artist called Jeffrey Vallance and the piece was called 'My FBI File'. In the US you can get an FBI file just by having correspondence with a Communist country. This was in the late eighties: he had had correspondence with people in China and Russia and so had a lengthy FBI file. But under the Freedom of Information Act, you could request to get a copy of your FBI file, so he did. He then blew up the most embarrassing part of his file, which was a police report describing an occasion when he had been found by the side of a road, lying in a ditch, babbling incoherently and sporadically trying to abuse himself! This is the kind of thing you wouldn't want your best friend to see, let alone your worst enemy, and he had blown it up into this great poster. But a funny thing happened, which interested me a great deal too in this area. It was that the person who read the poster felt acutely embarrassed; it seemed as if, somehow, the artist's own embarrassment slid off him and onto you and that by exposing a weakness, you could transfer it to somebody else. This idea seemed really interesting to me.

There was another piece in the show that was more about futility, which was actually called 'Coals to Newcastle' (1978). This was a piece by Chris Burden, where he went down to the US/Mexico border with several little rubber-band planes made out of very thin balsa wood and loaded on marijuana joints as bombs and flew them over the border to reverse the flow of drugs into Mexico! (Audience laughter) Perhaps the saddest piece was by Mike Kelley: there were two hand-woven cat blankets lying on the floor with a kitty dish, a feeding tray, some cat toys and then there was a cardboard box filled with a half-open bag of cat food and kitty litter. Then on the wall were condolence letters from vets for the deaths of these two cats. So this was a cat memorial! We all laugh, but it's very interesting that there's a huge industry in the United States of pet bereavement counselling. This is an area that is so socially belittled. I haven't had a pet since I was a little kid, but some of you may have pets and you know, when pets die, people get really upset. A lot of the time people are more emotionally attached to their pet than to humans in their lives, because you can get very close. So this piece, I thought, brought up a lot of interesting issues in terms of how you responded to it.

There was a very distinct emotional tenor to this show and it also addressed you in a kind of contradictory manner. It was about art that was somehow failing and yet succeeding, which was a very confusing concept for a lot of people and the show got criticised for various reasons. Some of this work really was pathetic. There was a piece where this one artist kept trying to send his work to various institutions like the Vatican and the Richard Nixon Museum, who rejected it, and then he would exhibit the rejected piece with the rejection letter. Sometimes the piece was rejected, not as a work of art, but in some other category! At the same time, it was very funny and the link between humour and cruelty was something that interested me: you start researching the history of humour and you find out that we have been laughing at people falling on banana skins for 3000 years! Other people have been wondering why this is so. One of my favourite explanations was by Elias Canetti, who linked this idea to the reason why, for a long time, it was impolite to smile at the dinner table: because the showing of our teeth originated when we would see helpless prey lying on the ground and we knew we could go over and take a bite out of it!

From this show, it was downhill from there! My next show was called 'Presenting Rearwards' (Rosamund Felsen Gallery, Los Angeles, 1991). I had originally been interested in art that somehow showed you its backside; that was in the corner so you couldn't really experience all of it. I hated the idea that when you walk in the gallery the whole set up was that you were in the middle of this Copernican universe where everything was laid out for you and you were the centre of it. I wanted work that somehow put you out of that, because I find it very boring to be in that position. But I couldn't find enough work at that time that was just about showing you the back of the work somehow. At the same time, I found tons of work that was literally about your backside and there was a good reason for this. I got interested in the sociology of anal iconography. In the 1980s something very interesting happened, in the United States at least, to the rear end. It became a kind of universal sex object. Obviously men and women both have rear ends, but suddenly the rear end was on the cover of magazines. Women would say, 'That guy's got a really cute butt.' That was a new thing at that point. But the thing about 'cute butts' for men and women was that they had to be hard. You weren't allowed to have a flabby butt! So there were countless magazine articles about how to firm up your butt. This is when Madonna and Janet Jackson started to do these videos on MTV that were about, 'This is how hard my butt is, watch me shake it!' (Audience laughter)

At the same time, these were the Reagan years in the US. In the late eighties, around '87, Ronald Reagan had colon cancer and they sent one of those in vitro cameras up his rear end into his colon and this was broadcast on national television. To me, this seemed like an incredible event in the history of our relationship to excrement and anality. I mean, Sartre had written of the rear end that it was this incredibly provocative symbol of our vulnerability: we walk around and we can't see it, but everybody else can. And when we're walking, it moves and we can't really control those movements! So here it is, this public face that we put forward that's totally out of control and that everyone else can see but we can't. It seemed the whole programme of the eighties was to get that wayward butt under control! No more wiggling, no more jiggling! And this seemed to be a metaphor for a lot of what was going on in terms of people's relationships to their bodies, an image-based culture. The Reagan thing seemed like evidence that the rear end had been so sanitised that it could now be broadcast on family prime-time television.

So I was interested in how artists seemed to be picking up on this, but from a really broad range of viewpoints. There was a Cindy Sherman piece which a lot of you probably know: it's a low angle view up this high school girl's dress; Cindy as a blonde high school girl. And her rear end is just exploded with huge, ugly boils; it's like a nightmare that has taken over your body; your unconscious is suddenly erupting. There was a wonderful piece by Paul McCarthy called 'Rear View': on a worktable there was this horrible-looking slab of a body made up of white plaster, and there was a hole in the rear end and you could see there was a light inside the body. When you walked over to the rear end and looked through it, there was a beautiful alpine village inside, just like Disney Land! To me, this was a reversal of Duchamp's 'Etant donnés'. Instead of looking through the architecture into this scene of some kind of strange sexual aftermath, you were looking through the rear end into this completely anal – in the sense of a completely cleansed-up – fantasy environment. There's something about Bavarian villages, at least in the US, that has been embraced as a symbol of hygiene: social hygiene, physical hygiene.

There was another piece by artist Richard Hawkins where he took pin-ups from gay porno magazines and drew on all the bodies to turn them into optical devices. So they were like periscopes, where you would look through someone's rear end and there was a line going up to their eye. There were a number of works that seemed to equate the eye and the anus; there must have been some kind of Bataille influence at that point! There was also work by an African artist where he put his treasured family, paternal and tribal face masks next to his rear end. Ora Rosenberg did these interesting pictures where she took the rear ends from porno magazines and printed them on rocks, which she then put in nature. So they were like these fragments of porn in nature: inside trees, in desert landscapes, and it was kind of fitting.

That show got a very strange response: some people found it extremely disturbing and just thought it was angry. I thought it was funny; well, I thought it was a mix. But I knew when I did it that it was a risk to do a show that was so narrow in terms of its subject matter, even though there were so many different points of view; sort of like curating a bird show or a cat show. But it was a risk I wanted to take. I thought the work was so different that it was worth doing.

Three or four years ago I did a show called 'The Scene of the Crime' which grew out of an interest in police photographs. Police photographs seemed to me like the first installation shot: they're always haunted by the sense of some previous action that occurred and as a viewer you have to reconstruct what happened there. And this seemed a metaphor for looking at a lot of contemporary art, and looking at art that normally wasn't considered together – like Jackson Pollock's splatter paintings – in a forensic framework. And linking that to installation art by later people; looking at photographers who photograph scenes of aftermath; at work that dealt in different ways with absent bodies, and where those works place your own body as a spectator, that's what I was interested in.

The last show I did was at the Serpentine Gallery, co-curated with Lisa Corrin ('The Greenhouse Effect', 2000). If you've ever been to the Serpentine in London, you know it's in the middle of Hyde Park and it's got these windows that look out onto the park. Whenever I've been to shows there, I've always thought that the views out the window were such an important part of the exhibition. So I wanted to do an exhibition where those views made sense as part of the exhibition. I got really tired of thinking an exhibition is 'about this' or it's 'about that'. I thought, why couldn't an exhibition just be about creating a place? So I had an idea of creating a kind of odd greenhouse, which would have, hopefully, some different rhetorical effects in terms of how you looked at things there. Some of the works in the show were very finely made objects, like insects and plants that were made by hand but looked completely real. Then there were other works that involved living things, but that looked completely fake. So at the most base level, there was this kind of lure to get people interested: they were standing for twenty minutes in front of an apple tree wondering how the artist made this, when in fact it was a real apple tree!

I always think it's useful to try to unsettle your viewer in some way, so they look at things differently. But I was also interested in the idea that works about nature probably tell us more about culture and how we frame things than any other kind of art. And it did kind of work as an environment. There were miniature models of Amazonian rainforests as well as experiential pieces. There was an Olafur Eliasson room where you walked in and it was raining ('your strange certainty still kept', 1996). The idea was hopefully to put the viewer, from piece to piece, in a slightly different position in terms of what your relationship to looking at this was, how you're reading it, from a fantastical thing to a factual position. There was a great piece by an artist named Rachel Berwick in the middle of the big dome ('May-por-é', 1998). This was a large structure with some live parrots in it who were speaking a language that no one had spoken for four hundred years, but that had been transcribed from a pair of parrots by a naturalist. They were the last parrots of an exterminated Amazonian tribe and the last 'people' who spoke this language. He (the naturalist) transcribed forty words of this language and the artist taught another pair of parrots the language again. You only saw them as shadows, because they were in this big aviary structure that was covered with a kind of canvas material. But you heard their words and you also heard a recording of their speaking and it was very hard to tell which was which. So you could circle around this; the parrots would move and their shadows would move, and you were never quite sure exactly what you were hearing or seeing. That was one of the things the show was about.

I must stop.

(Audience applause)

RICHARD GRAYSON:

This is going to be a really confused presentation, I can promise this before we start, because I'm in a curious situation where my curatorial practice has banged back and forth with my art practice.

This is a slide I've been carrying around since 1981. I was a student up here: not at this college but at the place which has since become a university (University of Northumbria). There was a group of us who were all terribly, terribly interested in live art. We managed to be interested in live art in spite of the fact that we couldn't see any. There didn't seem to be any going on; it was something that we read about. I think there was one particularly grainy Chris Burden catalogue. The only way out of this problem seemed to be to set up a place, not only for other artists to show, so we could see what they were doing, but for us to show as well. I don't know if anybody in this room has done this, but one feels particularly stupid doing a piece of performance art in an art school. It really doesn't feel as if it's got any resonance. So we needed a place where we could do our own stuff. We found a small room under a defunct Newcastle organisation called Spectro Arts Workshop, which has now become a car park behind the fire station, and we rented this place from Spectro for about £5 a week. Over a period of four years we (The Basement Group) put on

248 events by other artists and quite a number by ourselves.

At no point did we make any clear division between our work and other artists' work; what united it was 'performance', or that it was time-based basically. Sometimes we were asked to go on tour, so we'd go to France or, if we were less lucky, we'd go to Nottingham! If we went to Nottingham we'd invite a couple of French artists who had shown at The Basement to show with us. We were making, I suppose, a bit of a gang. I can't think of many art or curatorial practices analogous to this, but there are a lot of music practices that are analogous to it. This was really like a performance art version of the Lollapalooza festival, on a far smaller budget.

(Slides) This is a gloriously curatorially sound slide of a piece from many years ago, happening in a room somewhere! As you can see, it's a thinner me, scribbling words and phrases onto his chest with a texta-pen. Several years later I made a piece of fake documentation of this work, where the words seem to go into a sentence. You can see, 'Dear Richard, I think of you, I think of you, you prick, you have ruined my life.' In fact, the original performance made no sense at all, so I'm faking a narrative. This interest in narrative, narratives and fictions, fakings and re-modellings, has continued to inform both my art practice and my curatorial practice. I'm using curatorial practice here as a shorthand, and if I've got time I shall return to that later because it's not a phrase I particularly like, but I'm using it for ease of reference.

This is me as a recovering performance artist. This is the end of my performance career, with Michelle Luke, an Australian artist with whom I made a lot of work. Again, making rebuses, nearly making sense: it was up to the audiences to try and extract any sense from what was going on. Later still, I was using letters which I myself had received, usually some ten or fifteen years before, when you are in that period of your life when you're at your most romantic, when everything is significant because everything will 'add up', you're certain of this. At some point in your future there will be a biographer who wants to read these letters, so you keep them. You then reach a point in your future when you realise that the biographer is late! (Audience laughter) What I was doing here – these in a way are post-performative pieces – was projecting these letters onto the walls of spaces, hammer drilling them in and just leaving the space. This was not open to the public, but when the audience came in they just saw the detritus, the part of this message which implied another message, another narrative; one which you were forever denied but were allowed little glimpses or flashes of. It was up to you to construct the meaning. Not only could you feel the history of the pieces I'm making, but the history behind that history. Half-vandalism, half-sculpture, half-graffiti.

Other times it would be texts that I'd found. This is an old warehouse in South Australia that was about to be knocked down and this was a text that had been left by somebody saying, 'Helen, Steve, my keys are upstairs.' So I hammer-drilled this into the wall memorialising this exchange between whoever Helen was and whoever Steve was, and the unknown writer. A series of paintings came out of this. This is a rather alarming piece I found on the street. Australia was directly and actively involved with the Vietnam War. It didn't only give mental support; it sent people over there as well. This text reads, 'This return claims headaches, blackouts, loss of memory, violent temper, bad dreams, due to blown unconscious by enemy mortars, 1971. Continual dreams about contacts, 1973. There are no records of these symptoms in his S/docs. Would you please diagnose them?' This had been ripped in half and trampled into the floor by, I presume, the person whom the referral was made for. So I used this piece of found text; again, inferring stories and other narratives.

This is very specific to the Australian context. This is a letter given to me by a friend who's a Cypriot Turk, from his mother, who learned to write at the age of sixty, only so that she could write to her departed son. Australia is very much a land of immigration and emigration. And also, to us, unless we can read Cypriot-Turkish, when we read the word 'Allah' we understand it to mean one thing – the name of god – but that's a misunderstanding: in this letter it doesn't mean that at all. So we're extracting the wrong meaning out of this.

These themes are developing within my work. At that time I was also curating some stuff because somebody had given me a job, rather to my surprise. Themes seemed to be definitely emerging but at no point did I think, 'Wouldn't it be interesting to explore…?' or, 'Wouldn't it be interesting to look at…?' The themes often seem to be retrospective. You think, 'Oh, that's what we were thinking of,' when one looks back. I guess what I'm trying to say here is that many of my approaches when programming the Experimental Art Foundation (EAF) were intuitive, based only on reactions and thoughts rather than an overarching theme, or a need to say anything about a moment or movement in art. Most often it was as simple as liking what an artist does and asking them to make a work for the space. It was very rare that the work was determined. It was far more, 'Look, here's the space, do what you want with it,' providing a space and an opportunity for the artist to make new work. Then later you realise that, in fact, these shows do hang together in some sort of narrative or are linked because they have some common approaches, and that there was a level of thinking going on that you weren't quite aware of at the time. Other times it might be more pro-active, saying, for instance, 'Well, what is happening with artists who may define their practice as painting-based? What does that look like now? What are they thinking about?' Then getting on the phone to a bunch of artists who are working with painting and saying, 'Look, there's a gap, and this is the idea of the season, what do you want to do with it?' Very carefully giving determination and direction over to the artist, but at the same time, trying to put these events together in a way that may make some sort of sentence.

This was a piece called 'Works About the Real World' and it's about how we might understand the world around us. They're potato prints and they're all of those facts that surround us, that promise so much but that deliver so little; all they do is illuminate themselves: 'Freud could not read railway timetables,' 'Father's Day was invented by a woman.' This was an ongoing series. We think that they illuminate our understanding of this universe, but they don't at all.

This was a piece specific to certain narratives of 'a place'. This is a town square in the centre of Adelaide called Victoria Square. It turns out to be the symbolic heart of the totemic animal of the local Aboriginal people, the Miwi peoples. They gather there still. It's also called Victoria Square to immortalise the Great White Empress. So I did this flower piece – 'Victoria' is her signature there – taken from a watercolour. Upside down is the word 'kharna', which is the name of the Aboriginal nation and it's in the handwriting of a female elder of the peoples. I did this in a long process of negotiation as an English import dealing with the dispossessed Aboriginal structures. It was a very interesting and difficult exchange. We worked on this for six months and it had, for us, some satisfying outcomes.

This is a paperweight that my partner brought back from Paris. This was a project that I did with another artist called Steve Wigg where we blew it up to be ten times in size ('Triumph'). So this is about four meters high and it's made out of three tonnes of white clay. It's a lot smaller than the original Arc de Triomphe and a lot larger than the paperweight. It also aged a lot faster than the Arc de

Triomphe has done so far: clay uses ten per cent of its bulk when it's drying out.

Coming back to Ralph's accidents, a whole piece about accidents here. Transcribed onto the wall, this is an entire script of potential accidents, most of them slapstick accidents, some of them not. Lacan's death is in there somewhere.

This is a work by Joyce Hinterding ('Siphon'), who is an Australian artist I think I will be looking at quite seriously with a view to a future project. She's absolutely fascinated by electricity. This is a collection of Leiden jars, an early form of battery; you smell this work as much as anything. They're being charged up with thousands of volts and then they discharge into the air. That metal thing there is vibrating so the jars change their sound as they fill up with electricity. Suddenly there's this 'woosh' and you get that extraordinary tingle of electricity and then it all starts again. She's also found that if you put electricity through large drawings of electrical diagrams, the diagrams work as the thing they're meant to be describing. What I really like about this is that the work is both about it's own nature and about something else at the same time. It's locked into other structures and other patterns other than those of the art world.

The Campfire Group. At the EAF we were often putting together projects that looked at cultural representations and understandings of certain ideas. One time about ideas of 'law' and another time we made a season of exhibitions and talks about ideas of death ('600,000 Hours'). This is work from that season. The Campfire Group are white and black artists in Australia working together trying to bridge the different knowledges, articulating different things. This is a work by Lindy Lee, a Chinese-Australian artist, called 'Zilch Zilch Zilch Zero': thousands of ink stains plastered around the gallery space. Another Chinese-Australian artist, Hiram To, now based in Hong Kong, again in the death project. This is called 'The Skin

I'm In': a drum kit with empty clothes photographed onto it. These are images form another project that the EAF initiated ('Litteraria'), where two artists, Simryn Gill and Robert MacPherson, were given unlimited access to the collections and the knowledge in the South Australian Museum, which is a vast collection of minerals, nature etc. Robert Macpherson is, I think, a brilliant Australian artist. These are Toas, objects that are found around the Lake Ayre region of Australia. Nobody is sure if they are fake or if they have a function. They don't come into the record books until the nineteenth century, so some people think they may have been made by the Aboriginal peoples to exchange with missionaries for trade goods like flour. Other people think they do have a deeply symbolic use, nobody's ever quite sure. The artist also happens to think they are some of the most beautiful objects he's seen. Each Toa seems to represent a waterhole. What the artist did in this project was to represent the Toas, and then in the background he listed all the varieties of frog associated with that particular waterhole. So you had two closed systems of knowledge: the Toas, that we couldn't understand, and the Latin names and classifications of frogs that was, in a way, the white construction of those places that the Toas came from, which neither Aboriginal cultures nor, in fact, most of us, can now understand because we don't speak Latin.

This is the last painting from the last show I did and it's called, 'The Current Inability to Construct a Viable Alternative to Global Capitalism'. Whilst I was working on the painting, I was thinking about the exhibition I was working on, the work that my partner Suzanne Treister does and the work that Susan Hiller and lots of other people do, when the Sydney Biennale people asked me and thirty-two others to put in an outline of what one might think interesting if one was doing a Sydney Biennale. I sent off a deeply thought-through A4 sheet of paper saying it would be interesting to look at artists who are using models, descriptions, fantasies etc., in which to model alternatives and look at the way we might, or might not, understand the world. Perhaps it's particularly interesting at the moment, with the collapse of the command economies, that the sort of thing that anchored the alternative proposition into the political, into the real, has been removed. It's very difficult now to see clearly a believable alternative to the current grey morass of global capitalism. The other reason it seemed to be interesting at this time to be thinking about this sort of thing was the effect that the information technologies are having on our cultural modellings and our own personal understandings. We can now go into spaces, any of us in this room, and claim, and be believed to be, twenty-three stone men, women, soldiers, nazis, whatever, and be operational in that persona. So in the widest way the project is going to be looking at ideas of the 'fantastic', not as some romantic Dungeons and Dragons expression, but as a space where cultures can talk to themselves, test alternatives.

The next Sydney Biennale is being done very much, not as a curators' gig, but as an artists' gig, I think, whereby it's not claiming to be diagnostic, it's just looking at certain things that might be interesting. It's going to be open and discursive. I'm making the choices but I've got a 'suggestion panel' rather than a selection panel, which includes Ralph (Rugoff) and Susan (Hiller) and a Hungarian artist called Janos Sugar. We've been batting around ideas, suggestions; it's a long, discursive process. I suppose this comes back to the my earlier point: a slight unease about being described as a curator. I see it more as a programmer or whatever you're doing when you're running an artist-run space, which isn't quite curation, it's something slightly different. Perhaps it's a bit more 'Lollapalooza'. That's it.

(Audience applause)

SUSAN HILLER:

Both of these extremely interesting talks have been quite
personal and indicate that neither Ralph nor Richard
would define themselves as curators in any traditional
sense. I'd like to start things off with a question about that
very point. At the very first one of these sessions that we
had, I said, perhaps provocatively, that in a sense curators
have usurped the role of artists in many instances. While
I hope we're passed that point of the great curator who
doesn't even bother to list the artists in the exhibition, it
still seems very clear to me, as an artist who has organised a couple of exhibitions, that the curator is in a different position to that of the artist. So if you don't call it
curating, what do you call it, because there's a filter
system and you're at the top of it? I know that Richard
curates as a visual artist and a writer and Ralph curates as
a writer, but is that really any different from what we think
curators do anyway?

RALPH RUGOFF:

I think when I'm curating, I don't know whether being a
writer affects what I do, but I'm definitely acting as a
curator. To me, there are lots of roles curators play. There
is some really pretentious rhetoric around what curators
do. One of our leading contemporary curators said, not
long ago, that we really need to raise the level of curating
to the complexity of the novel! This is not something I feel
as a personal ambition of mine, but I look back in this very
old fashioned way to the original meaning of the term
'curate': the idea that a curator is someone who takes
care of things. To me, the idea of taking care of a work of
art means to show it in a context where it's somehow
going to be alive, to be allowed to do what it does well. A
lot of work I see in institutions doesn't do that; it's actually
moribund. There's a lot of stinky, corpsey work lying
around even contemporary art centres, because it's not

doing what it should be doing. I think one really weird thing when you make a lot of studio visits is that you suddenly discover that, for some reason, a lot of work looks better in someone's studio than it ever does when it winds up in a gallery. There's a whole group of curators who feel that what's to blame is the architecture of the gallery or the institution of the museum. I think that's only part of the story. I think a curatorial premise can also prepare you mentally to look at the work in one way or another that might make it more interesting. So, to me that's a job description. Zoos have curators: the person who runs the collection of a zoo is called a curator and if you don't take care of the monkey's properly, they die! I feel it's a completely comparable situation.

SUSAN HILLER:

Richard, it was quite interesting that your talk didn't really emphasise the programming policies you must have undertaken and defined while you were running the Experimental Art Foundation, which is a large, publicly funded art space in Australia.

RICHARD GRAYSON:

This links to that use of the word 'programming'. For a long time I described myself as a programmer rather than a curator, because I don't think I've got the skills that a curator of reptiles in the zoo has, to be honest. In as much as the curator of reptiles in the zoo, if something small and green and prickly is brought to it can say, 'Oh yes, that's Bufo Bufo Bufari, it lives in South America and this one's been dead for two years.' (Audience laughter) And I think, actually, as a curator in the British Museum you can do that, but when you're working with contemporary art, it's a lot more fluid. I don't feel I've failed if somebody comes to me with the work of a terribly well established

Estonian artist from 1930 and says, 'Who's that by?' and I don't know. It's just not within my remit. So I've always been happier with the word 'programmer', which is fine when you're doing it through time, which a lot of the EAF stuff was: 'group shows' that didn't happen through space, they happened through time. One would choose the artist, they would do a large studio project and then another artist would perhaps be looking at the same theme.

'Programming' does fit that, as does 'facilitator': it's where you are facilitating the production of new work, which I think is terribly important. In a way, it was these slightly random themes that determined the programming policy of the Experimental Art Foundation in particular. One year I seem to remember getting terribly interested in cultural representations and understandings of death. I thought, 'Hey, it might be interesting to speak to some artists.' All of those works were commissioned. So I suppose in that instance you are a bit more like a theatre producer. It's lots of things, and in my understanding of what a curator is, it isn't anything like what the curator of classical antiquities or frogs is doing.

SUSAN HILLER:

We did name this series 'The Producers', not only because it's personally one of my favourite movies, so it was an ironic intention to some extent, but it is probably a better word than 'curating', isn't it, because you're enabling a production to occur, that wouldn't occur without you?

RICHARD GRAYSON:

I also think, coming back to your introductory comments, one of the things about the curator getting more power, is that when you've got your curator hat on, rather than your artist hat, it's significantly easier to raise money. If you write to somebody as an artist, you're waiting for a very long time, whereas there are actually structures set up around curators, for want of a better word. So it's easier for me, if I'm called a director of an Experimental Art Foundation, to raise money for artists, than it is either for them or me as an artist. I'm slightly out of touch with what's happening in the UK at the moment, but I believe that individual art grants have nearly evaporated, whilst if you're an organisation or whatever, there is funding available. Therefore it's more behoven upon those institutions, if they're going to do anything useful, to actually facilitate new productions.

RAPLH RUGOFF:

There's a difference between an institutional curator and a curator. I just took the first job in my life six months ago and before that, I'd curated as a freelance person. Trying to raise money as a freelance curator is probably even harder than trying to raise money as an artist.

RICHARD GRAYSON:

No, I disagree

RALPH RUGOFF:

There are no grants available for freelance curators. Believe me, I've checked!

RICHARD GRAYSON:

There were grants in Australia for freelance curators. Come to Australia!

SUSAN HILLER:

You've both worked inside as well as outside major institutions. (To Ralph Rugoff) How do you find the situation of working within and on behalf of the institution that you're now actually running in San Francisco?

RALPH RUGOFF:

It is totally different. I think whatever critical thoughts I've
had before about people working in institutions, I now have
to modify. Before, I only did an exhibition when I had an
idea I felt I really wanted to see as an exhibition and that
came out of a particular thinking process. But now I can't
spend eighteen months thinking about an exhibition,
because I've got to put on nine or twelve a year, although
I don't have to curate all of them. I do think that an exhibition is an exhibition; it's not a production. A production,
I think, is fine for theatrical things. I like the word exhibition.
I like the specificity of 'exhibition', because I think going to
an exhibition is a very specific sort of experience. I think the
gallery is a very specific visual technology and these are
the things, if you're organising exhibitions in art spaces,
that you have to deal with.

RICHARD GRAYSON:

I don't think I'm disagreeing with any of that. It's just my
feeling that we need a new word or neologism that doesn't
conflate the curator of the past or the curator of the British
Museum or the reptile house, with what people are doing
when they're working with contemporary art.

RALPH RUGOFF:

I think people do many different things when they're curating. There are people who curate historical shows; there
are people who like to do surveys. There are people who
see the most important thing they do as trying to enshrine a
group of artists in the canon that we supposedly got rid of.
This month at MoCA in Los Angeles, Paul Schimmel is
curating a show called 'The Global Academy' – that was
its original name – which is looking at artists from London,
Los Angeles, New York, Germany and Japan who all made
a big splash two years out of art school.[1] He feels it's really

[1] 'Public Offerings', Los Angeles Museum of Contemporary Art, 2001

important to get these artists in historical perspective now, before they turn thirty-five I guess! So there are all kinds of agendas, all kinds of things people are doing as curators. I don't think it's possible to generalise. I think one thing I've tried to do, which a lot of people don't, is to look at issues outside the art world, whether they're psychological, emotional, social or political issues, through curating a show. Because also when I curate a show, I feel it's very important that the catalogue is where those kinds of things are talked about as well. There are a lot of great shows that are only about things that are of concern to the art world and those within the art world, but my own interest is in between the two.

SUSAN HILLER:

You've both transplanted yourselves to and from various places. (To Richard Grayson) When you became the director of an institution, you were not in your so-called native land. (To Ralph Rugoff) You're back in the United States, and I just wondered how that travelling through different geographical worlds inflects on what you're doing? Because again, one of the claims made nowadays by institutional curators at least, is that they have an overview, that all information is completely available, they know what's happening everywhere. That always seemed to me, speaking as an artist, to be an incredibly silly position. I can understand how it might feel that way as one shuffles mentally through a profusion of facts, but of course, in the end, judgement remains completely subjective. To set up a totalising agenda usually hides its tokenism. There is no other way than using your own subjective judgement, and I wondered if you feel travelling disrupts that kind of procedure?

RALPH RUGOFF:

There is a species of curator who spends half of his or her life on an aeroplane, is a 'frequent flyer curator'. The great currency that they possess is that they can tell you who the top ten artists are in some country you've never visited in your life and may never visit. But they know; they have this information. They curate big biennales, which tend to take on a United Nations style approach and that seems to be their only virtue: that they include somebody from almost every country, rather than having any aesthetic ideas. That ethical idea is what those things are about. To me that's not an interesting context. I think you can know about everything in the world and not necessarily know what it means or understand it in a meaningful way. I think a lot of interesting cultural developments, whether it's rock music or literary scenes or art scenes, develop locally. They develop in little laboratory-type situations in specific communities where those people are bouncing around ideas to reach a certain kind of level, of atmosphere, pressure or whatever, and something starts to generate out of that. You can do the same things with exhibitions. Me going back some place means that it's further to come here and keep up with what's going on, but it means I'm closer to Los Angeles now, which also has a very vital art scene. I'm not an exponent of regionalism, but I think there's a local dynamic that can be very interesting and that often gets overlooked in our focus on globalism right now.

RICHARD GRAYSON:

I think it's something to do with the speed of travel as well, isn't it? If you're a slow traveller, as I have been, rather than rushing back and forth, you become more aware of these laboratories and therefore the idea of this canon becomes increasingly impossible and ridiculous. I know perfectly well that there are five, six or seven really interesting artists who will never be embraced into this biennale world; they will never go international. It's almost as if there's this structural thing where each place produces analogues: there's somebody doing this sort of work in an interesting way, somebody doing that sort of work in an interesting way. Some of these people will get picked up, some of them won't.

I've just come back from Arco (International Contemporary Art Fair, Madrid, 2001) where, through some sort of mischance of programming, I got put onto a board with a lot of the frequent flyer biennale curators. The thing which came across to me very strongly – and this is not me being parochial or proudly regional – was that a lot of the debates about diversity, regionalism, ideas of the periphery and ideas of the centre, were actually far more advanced in a seemingly semi-hick, semi-Anglo Saxon place like Australia, because they've been on the receiving end of the sentence for so long. Whilst these people were actually of many different races and cultures, they definitely saw themselves as being of 'the centre'. They were therefore still speaking 'for' others who seemingly couldn't speak for themselves, and they were talking about the biennale as a utopia, which comes back to this idea of the United Nations. It struck me as terribly naïve and annoying. I must admit to being surprised because I'm not the sort of person who has been to many biennales, I've never been to these think tanks or panels. I was actually expecting to have a good time and to meet lots of really bright people who would tell me lots of inter-esting things. Instead I got furious, in a quiet, British sort of way: I muttered! But it was an education.

SUSAN HILLER:

I was thinking more about slow travelling, since I know you have both lived in other places for quite long periods of time. I wasn't suggesting that you were frequent flyer

type people. Although sometimes that's fun and necessary, and it can be very informative of course. I was
reflecting on what happened to me when I came to this
country a long time ago, and found there was a completely
different art history that at first I thought was so silly; I just
couldn't believe it! 'What, they're not interested in the
same painters that I'm interested in?' How could this be,
and who were these artists they were talking about all the
time? I was completely in the dark. I went through all
those attitudes, from lack of interest and disdain to, 'Oh
my God, I better find out' and now, of course, I'm hooked
on these people that no one in the United States has ever
heard of. That kind of thing obviously shifts one's perspective on the way you look at contemporary developments.
I think one of the things you both have in common is that
you've lived for long periods of time in other places.
I wondered how one would begin to think about those
very different sets of histories, which also imply different
kinds of judgements on contemporary developments?

RICHARD GRAYSON:

I do think I've become more aware of this analogous thing.
One of the weird discoveries was that there is an equiva-
lent of a painter like Ivor Hitchens in every single country;
somebody who did slightly semi-abstract landscapes and
is seen as important within the local context because it's a
bridge between representation and abstraction. But the
number of them out there is quite stunning! There were at
least five Ivor Hitchens in Australia. It's not an entirely flip
point, because many of the commentaries, discussions
and thought processes are going to be shared, but at the
same time, they are crucially different. It's just made me
less willing to accept the canon in practically every single
way. I think that's why I get really snooty with some of the
activities and carryings-on of some contemporary curatorial practices, because they tend to be self-aggrandising

and essentially profoundly silly somewhere along the line. They're actually doing it for themselves rather than for anyone else. That makes me sound far more moral than I've ever wanted to sound: it's getting to me, I think!

RALPH RUGOFF:

When I first came here I had a similar experience but it was involving contemporary art. I couldn't believe that through all the early years of Rachel Whiteread, no one mentioned Bruce Nauman! The Chapman Brothers themselves openly said, 'Yes, we've taken all our stuff from Charlie Ray and Paul McCarthy', but critically, the critics here didn't seem to know what that meant. The connections between Damien Hirst and Jeff Koons were also things that were largely unexplored. It seemed like there was a particularly sort of island mentality in England maybe, because there were also lots of German influences that didn't seem to be generally acknowledged. If you look at Gerhard Richter's colour-chart paintings and then you look at Damien Hirst's paintings, there's not a huge difference. So I wanted to curate a show called 'The Anxiety of Influence', to borrow Harold Bloom's title. I was actually talking to Tate Britain about doing this when I left; I thought I'd leave that mess behind me! It was not going to be a show that would make me very popular, but part of my interest in doing an exhibition like this was to show that actually, everybody who used a given idea ended up doing something different with it. So there's an anxiety of influence that if your work is too close to someone else's, then maybe there's a crisis of meaning.

There was one year where I saw six or seven videos of artists dancing in their studios wearing headphones. I think Gillian Wearing did a piece like this, and Peter Land. I thought you could have this great room in the exhibition, with eight people dancing around wearing their headphones and you would think this was one piece!

I really thought that what you would see was not just the similarity and the influence, but also difference, because to me if you get rid of that idea of originality, you no longer have to think, 'There are five Ivor Hitchens in Australia.' I think you can look at things in a slightly different way.

SUSAN HILLER:

It's an interesting issue, because when Richard says 'five Ivor Hitchens', we know what he means. I've always maintained that art history isn't a narrative of somebody doing something and a lot of other people being influenced by it. It's a case of simultaneous developments and thoughts, and it proves that basically we're all just molecules in the great bloodstream of the universe. It seems to me that the economic system inflects in such a way as to impose singularity and pre-eminence. When you have been teaching enough years and you look across different art schools, you see that there was 'the year of the balloon', not just the year of the dancing with headphones. And these people were not in touch with one another at all, but something much more interesting was happening, which is different people working on problems that are coming up on the thought horizon, if you like. So the works are very similar and they are also very different, but this idea doesn't seem to have been grasped very strongly by public structures, because there's still that older idea of influence and followers and so forth.

RALPH RUGOFF:

Part of it was talking to a lot of those English artists who would say, 'I didn't even know about that other work.' Douglas Gordon would say, 'I never knew about Warhol's 'Empire',' and you go, 'How could he say that? How could you go through art school and not have some knowledge of it?' There are so many art schools in the world right now, so many art students, so many people thinking about similar issues, making work, that I think that old idea of originality and pre-eminence...yes, it's tied to the market, but I also think it's tied to some idea of art that steps outside of its time, above its time, to transcend it. But if you start thinking in terms of local effect – what effect does this work have in this context, at this time? – it's a very different kind of discussion.

QUESTION

You're somewhat derisory about artists having a slightly insular view. Isn't this one of the jobs of the curator, to break this down?

RALPH RUGOFF:

Ideally, yes. Absolutely!

RICHARD GRAYSON:

But curators can sometimes support the artist's insular view as well. For reasons totally beyond me there is, or has been, an Australian Anthony Caro, who is not Anthony Caro at all. But the only person who could tell the difference between them would be Anthony Caro! There have been curators within the country who have helped establish, place and justify this work, and not really mentioned the fact that this stuff looks like Anthony Caro. Because in many ways, this work does the things in the culture and occupies the space that Caro does in British art history. The curators allowed it to happen, in a way. What I'm talking about is how the curator, rather than being educative and saying 'no', as often happens, says 'yes', because they want to establish their sphere as well. They want to become an expert on Australian art of a certain time because then they can get a job, so certain boats aren't rocked, certain things are allowed to stand at face value.

RALPH RUGOFF:

There are also popularity contests going on. Certain museums are under pressure to show, say British art, because there was a big buzz around it. The only reason a museum got interested in doing this show I was talking about ('The Anxiety of Influence'), was because of the split between Tate Modern and Tate Britain. Tate Britain was suddenly trying to think of ways to link contemporary British art to an international context, so that they could show some international artists in Tate Britain! So, it was only out of that desperation that the institution got interested in this idea.

SUSAN HILLER:

I think that there are many different factors going on in all of this and I think we've named some of them: aspects such as prestige and building up histories. For example, a few years ago I really blotted my copybook with a very influential journalist/art critic who had a sort of crush on Lucien Freud! I was saying to this critic that it was an approach to representation that I wasn't really sympathetic to and I mentioned the name Phillip Pearlstein, who is an American artist who makes it look easy. This critic hasn't spoken to me since, because there's this old fashioned idea of the great artist and you're not allowed to compare, discuss, analyse or in any way dissect in terms of these issues we're pulling out rather humorously: similarity, difference, local effect, national effect, the intersection of the market, sheer good luck, bad luck, those kinds of things. Personally, speaking as an artist, I think it's very important for artists to recognise those factors and not be filled with despair if the hand of fate doesn't shove them into one of these odd positions which, as you say, can get deconstructed very quickly.

RICHARD GRAYSON

It's also very poignant though when you come across it and perhaps you come across it more when you get closer to being a frequent flyer, I don't know. But walking through this art fair the other day – and I still haven't decided what to do about this – in one of the groovier English galleries there was a painting which was coming out of a very specific process in which a lot of the sense of the painting lies. And I will be writing about an artist in Australia who has been doing this for ten years. When I saw it I thought, 'What's he doing showing in this gallery?' The only difference was that one was using gloss paint, one was using matt paint. And I know which one will get in the history books in the end; it'll be the one who was showing in the groovy gallery. The person in Australia will become the southern hemisphere version or will get terribly fed up, give up and do something else. And it's quite tough as an artist: unless you're very, very good, you're lucky if you have two or three really good ideas. And when you've had a good idea and it's really going somewhere, and then somebody else comes along and gets the recognition because they are closer to the mechanisms of recognition – the writers, the curators – there's nothing you can do about it, but it's very awkward.

SUSAN HILLER:

It's almost an ethical problem that isn't often addressed by those who curate, produce, select or make decisions. Really the issue is how to shift the defining worldview that creates these strange situations. Because any selection is arbitrary to an extent; all classifications are incomplete and the people who say, 'I've seen the five best artists in Lagos,' don't usually care to discuss what 'best' means, at least not with artists. In fact, if as an artist, you open up this discussion, this tends to guarantee your exclusion from whatever art community represents itself at biennales. It would be a real move forward to have this kind of critique going on a lot more on the curatorial side.

RALPH RUGOFF:

A curator doesn't just select works of art; this is what I was saying when I brought up the zoo thing. It's about providing a habitat. (To Richard Grayson) I think you're thinking of the natural historian when you talk about someone who can say, 'this is this type of tortoise or this species,' or whatever.

RICHARD GRAYSON:

No, I'm talking about the curator of reptiles!

RALPH RUGOFF:

In any case, you still have to make sure the reptile can stay alive. When I first curated this 'Just Pathetic' show, it was in a couple of different galleries and part of the tension there was that this work that was so pathetic was for sale. So that Mike Kelley piece, the cat memorial, imagine selling these things that belonged to your cats! That was part of the piece, its content. That piece was later bought by someone and donated to the Museum of Contemporary Art (Los Angeles) and later appeared in an exhibition of their recent acquisitions. In the context of this spanking new museum, which looked like a really high-end car dealership, the piece didn't work. I went and saw it and I was shocked, because I love this piece. Suddenly it wasn't doing what it had done before; it just wasn't functioning. That's because that piece isn't just an autonomous piece: it's relating to what's around it, the conditions of viewing as well as the physical space. All these are things you have to think about as a curator.

SUSAN HILLER:

Is that an extension or another dimension of the problem, which artists all know about intimately, of photographic or video documentation: some work looks terrible in photographs and it kills the work, whereas other people make work that looks great in photographs? What I'm getting at is that artists know these things, but it seems very difficult to transmit that knowledge to many curators and that's the reason that a lot of artists go into curating, I think. But it doesn't usually become something they do a lot of, because of all the organisational problems that you talked about.

RICHARD GRAYSON:

I also think, coming back to the confusion – or 'confusions' – of the curator thing, and why curators aren't sorting out these debates or suggesting them, is perhaps because of the blurriness of the terms curator, producer, whatever. Many of us are behaving far more as say, an André Breton would have done, or an Apollinaire, where you're actually trying to generate, create or propel a certain school. It's almost a return to an old modernism, which I find sort of entertaining, where every movement had a manifesto. Now, rather than the manifesto being done by Marinetti, it has been written by the curator in a slightly different sort of way. I do think that muddies the water, sometimes in an interesting way, vis-à-vis, 'How is the curator speaking? Who is the curator speaking to? What is the purpose of that speech?'

RALPH RUGOFF:

There are some curious, rigid distinctions that still hold. Jim Shaw is an artist who collects these paintings that he finds in thrift stores. They're a fantastic collection of paintings that seem to be deviant strains of every form of modern art you could imagine. They were all made by

'Sunday painters', and by comparison, they make painting that you see in the art world look very narrow in terms of its subject matter. He's only interested in representational painting. He's had several shows – there was one recently at the ICA in London – where he shows this collection. Now he doesn't consider this a work of art, this is not his work; he's a curator. A lot of artists would say that this is their piece. His feeling is really that there are individual people who painted all these things and he's collected them and that's his role. I've occasionally guessed lectured on the Royal College of Art's curating programme and when they (the students) are planning their exhibition, they often have a lot of anxiety about, 'Well, if we presented it this way, wouldn't we be working too much like artists and then we'd be out of our place?' So there seems to be a fair amount of anxiety about these two roles and maintaining some difference, that I think has a lot to do with the question of authorship. For all the bravado of even the most egomaniacal curators I know, I don't think any of them really make the claim of authorship, outside of one or two really extreme examples!

SUSAN HILLER:

That doesn't seem so strange to me really, because if you're making a painting, you don't claim that you've ground your own colours, at least not any more; but you select your colours and the combinations of the things that you do, the choices you make, are definitive. You did say Ralph, that you wanted to create a greenhouse in the Serpentine. I thought that was fascinating and a very beautiful description of what you did in that exhibition: you selected artists whose ideas and techniques were sympathetic with that overall concept. I'm not saying curators are artists, I'm just saying that it's a creative practice, basically.

RALPH RUGOFF:

I think I was an interior decorator, actually!

COMMENT FROM AUDIENCE:

I always thought the Serpentine was a greenhouse, before it was renovated....

RALPH RUGOFF:

Exactly! I was just trying to draw that latent content out. It was a teahouse.

QUESTION (SUNE NORDGREN):

Could I be very selfish? One of the reasons we bring distinguished guests here is to get some feedback. I really appreciate Richard saying, for example, that the Sydney Biennale this year will be an 'artists' gig'. That's nice. And Ralph talking about taking care of monkeys, which is a nice attitude towards curating! I also picked up on the point you made about peripheries and being 'local'. So why not stay local then? What we are trying to do at BALTIC is to be local and international at the same time. I just wanted to hear whether you could support that. Is it possible to do?

RALPH RUGOFF:

Yes, I think that's the balance you want to achieve. I think it's a very tricky thing. I mean, the classic thing you often see is international artists being invited to do site-specific works or works that somehow respond to a given environment. They're supposed to go somewhere for two months, have the complete culture of the area sussed out, and make a piece that responds to it. To me, that's usually pretty disastrous as a process. But at the same time, I think you could probably choose an international artist whose work reflects things that are of local concern and that's a way to deal with it.

RICHARD GRAYSON:

I feel that often what happens is gloriously outside of one's control, in a way. Newcastle, I remember, used to have quite a strong programme of public sculpture where somebody would come up and build something vaguely boat-shaped and then go, and that was their way of reacting to what was happening with the shipyards. That doesn't work. At the same time, in South Australia, just by chance, we brought over Henri Chopin who was a furious, glorious, sixties and seventies sound poet. We had people staying on the floor to be near him – it was a very weird experience! It did alter, on some sort of level, the way people were thinking about art. South Australia was in the grip of extreme postmodernism at the time; everything was without meaning; any statement, any narrative was de facto too complicated and we were in a vortex of the moronic. Then you have Henri Chopin, believing it was still possible to destroy civilisation by making strange noises very loudly; that there was an agenda and that art was about something that was outside and greater than the work's own self reference, very romantic. It really hit a smallish town with an intelligent community like a shell, but one could never have predicted this. I think you can get these exchanges going but they're bloody difficult to plan! If somebody had said to me, 'Do you want Henri Chopin to visit your local community?' I'd have said, 'No, my local community won't understand what he's saying. He's French and very loud!' When these things occur, you do feel that something worthwhile has happened which is not to do with the organisation, but just something worthwhile generally. So yes, it can be done, but I've no idea how you can ensure that it happens!

SUSAN HILLER:

But can it happen the other way round? Can the local become a springboard for the international, in a different way? I mean reciprocity is a nice idea, isn't it?

RALPH RUGOFF:

The local can become international: look at the Manchester music scene for example.

RICHARD GRAYSON:

It depends on one's position with nodes of power or one's rhetoric about exchange, or whatever. What often happens is that you just end up with an export scheme, so that people leave. Every town, every city, is going to produce some really groovy people. All but the strongest get really fed up with just being groovy and being there and supporting the locale. So after a while, after about five or six years you think, 'Sod this, I'm off.' Especially if there is someone at the other end saying, 'I've got a wonderful residency in Pasadena for you for four years.'

RALPH RUGOFF:

Also, locales are perhaps not as different as they used to be: with the spread of mass media, chain stores and fast food restaurants, you could be in almost any city in the world.

RICHARD GRAYSON:

I don't know whether that's true actually. I thought that a lot about Australia; they have the same TV programmes, 'Dad's Army' for God's sake! I thought, 'This culture's going to be very similar,' but after a while of course, it's not. It's very foreign, very weird.

RALPH RUGOFF:

Bu there are similar influences I think. You're still dealing with a Gap ad in Australia, America, the UK.

RICHARD GRAYSON:

Absolutely. You can see 'Seinfeld' in practically every country on this globe at the moment. But I don't know, in a way, how pervasive that is. It is pervasive but I don't know how flattening it is.

COMMENT FROM AUDIENCE:

But you're seeing it from a different position to a person in another country; it's not the same ad.

RALPH RUGOFF:

I grew up in New York City and every time I go back there's a new phalanx of chain stores that have replaced older, smaller, independent stores, and it does change the character of the city: it's becoming more and more like a suburban mall. That, I think, makes it like other cities.

RICHARD GRAYSON:

Just to pick up on your early point about biennales, I actually think this is exactly what a lot of the biennales are doing. It's globalisation at its worst. They think they're embracing diversity, but what they're actually doing is commodifying and flattening diversity. That's why you can go to a biennale in one place and it looks uncannily like your cityscape: you've got the Gaps, the Banana Republics.

You say that a biennale presents artists that are very well known; for you maybe, but the local people may never have heard of them.

RICHARD GRAYSON:

That's the other difficult equation. In Adelaide I wanted to bring people in so that there could be a difficult, proper exchange between artists that you don't get from magazines, etc. I hoped that there would be an interesting exchange between the 'local' and artists from elsewhere. That can happen with a biennale but what often happens, which makes me more pessimistic about it, is that every biennale will have some local artists from the area or country where the show is. In the next biennale, somewhere else, you'll have the usual suspects plus 'the local'. Now, the local doesn't travel, they are just in the biennale of their country; they hardly ever get picked up to go to say, a Taipei or a Kathmandu or a Limerick or a Sydney Biennale. It's quite funny looking at artists in Australia: some of them have been in five Sydney Biennales because it's been going a long time but they haven't got onto the international biennale circuit, because they're not part of that group. (To questioner) So your point is true, but there's also something rather more complex going on which I can't quite put my finger on, but it's not working in the mix and match way that people think it should.

RALPH RUGOFF:

It's difficult, because even in our discussions about what could possibly be in the Sydney Biennale, there was talk about, 'This person's in every biennale but they haven't actually been shown in Sydney yet, so maybe they should be.' Obviously, when you're making an exhibition, you have a local audience and you want to create an exhibition that will have some appeal to a local audience. But at the same time, you want to be participating in a larger discussion with everyone who's making exhibitions and thinking about these questions.

RICHARD GRAYSON:

Yes, and that's where I think it just becomes very difficult. For in addition to the local audience, there is an audience that does fly in to have a look and then flies out. So what happens when your audience becomes as slippery as your show?

RALPH RUGOFF:

Sometimes it's just the idea of a show.

RICHARD GRAYSON:

What I used to like about being a student here in Newcastle, was that we'd all sit there reading descriptions of work we hadn't seen, and being good art students, we were ripping it off something ferocious! You'd find out a year later that, in fact, you'd misunderstood it or that your thing was from a different planet. We would get our information from those old black and white copies of Flash Art. You had a little sort of black thing of what might have been Boetti standing in the middle of a field but you had no idea. So we'd all go and stand in the middle of fields and get it totally wrong! I do think that this working solely on an idea could be a genuinely interesting dialogue between the local and the international; creative misunderstanding. It would be nice if it happened more with shows actually, if there was another take, another version. So you would have the 'Just Pathetic' of the Ukraine by somebody who hadn't seen Ralph's show. They'd probably come up with quite a nice thing.

SUSAN HILLER:

Unfortunately it's time to draw this to a close. I want to thank both our speakers very, very much for an exceptionally frank and interesting event. I hope they won't mind continuing the discussion informally over a glass of wine, because I know a lot of people want to talk with them.

(Audience applause)

THE PRODUCERS: CONTEMPORARY CURATORS IN CONVERSATION

15 MARCH 2001, UNIVERSITY OF NEWCASTLE, DEPARTMENT OF FINE ART

LISA CORRIN AND JON BEWLEY IN CONVERSATION CHAIRED BY ANDY THOMSON

ANDREW BURTON:

Welcome to the eighth in our series of discussions in which we invite distinguished curators to come to Newcastle in the lead-up to the opening of BALTIC, to discuss issues of contemporary curatorship as part of the series 'The Producers', organised by Susan Hiller. Our two speakers tonight are firstly, Lisa Corrin, chief curator at the Serpentine Gallery, London, until July, when she's moving to Seattle to take up the post of Deputy Director for Art / Jon and Mary Shirley Curator of Modern and Contemporary Art at the Seattle Art Museum. Lisa's been at the Serpentine for four years, since the refurbishment of the gallery. She curated the first UK show of Felix Gonzales-Torres, which I'm sure a lot of people here will have seen, and currently, 'Give and Take', which is split between the Serpentine and the V & A. At the V & A, there are fifteen artists who have works dispersed around the museum, including some phenomenal Marc Quinn sculptures in the first room.

A lot of you will know our second speaker, Jon Bewley, as he's based in Newcastle and is co-director, with Simon Herbert, of Locus+. Locus+ have a very strong record of commissioning, mostly temporary artworks, both in the region but also throughout the country. For example, the Anya Gallacio piece ('Two Sisters', Minerva Pier, Kingston upon Hull), which was part of Artranspennine in 1998 but also Wendy Kirkup's piece ('Echo', 2000), that was shown at the Centre for Life in Newcastle. Locus+ also have a strong record on publications, and have just published a book on artist Richard Wright.

The proceedings are going to be chaired tonight by Andy Thomson, who has joined the Fine Art Department this year. He has come from RMIT University in Melbourne, Australia, and is an artist. He works collaboratively, which is a new and exciting thing for the Department, and he's shown extensively in Australia and also in Korea. (To Andy Thomson) Over to you.

ANDY THOMSON:

First of all I'd like to ask Lisa to make her presentation and afterwards Jon will make his, and then we'll have some discussion. During the presentations, I'd ask you to consider the kinds of questions you'd like to put to the two speakers. It's very important that we have a dialogue, as well as that they talk to one another.

LISA CORRIN:

I became a curator in a very roundabout way; I never intended to be a curator of contemporary art. I actually started off studying fourteenth-century Italian sculpture and though I did also have a degree in theory and contemporary art, the last place I thought I'd wind up was curating exhibitions. I was sure I was going to be an academic.

How I became a curator is really very simple: I was asking the right questions in the wrong place, which was graduate school. Then I took some time off and happened to be introduced to George Ciscle, a former teacher and gallerist who initially dreamt of founding a forty thousand square foot white cube in Baltimore. George asked me to be the assistant director, even though I'd never done an exhibition in my life or even worked in a museum. Neither George nor I had been shaped by working inside mainstream institutions. This actually gave us an advantage. We were already thinking outside 'the box'. We immediately started asking questions like 'what is a museum?' when we developed The Contemporary, a museum with neither a space nor a collection. The Contemporary presented two exhibitions a year in spaces ranging from institutions that we sequestered – along with their staff and their permanent collection – to projects in other temporary sites that were designed to add context and meaning to the work of contemporary artists that would not be possible within the context of a traditional modern art museum. As a result of developing The Contemporary with George, context, that is, how a site adds meaning to a work of art and how a work of art adds meaning to a site, became central to my thinking. As someone recently said to me, 'Context for you is the engine of invention.'

The Contemporary also got me thinking about self-reflexivity: how to get the audience to ask questions along with the artist, the curator, and the institution, about the definition of art: what is an artist, what is an audience and in fact, what is a museum? George and I felt it critical that we be as transparent as possible about the process of making exhibitions as well as about the artistic process. Artist residencies made that process more available to the community and were a steady component of our projects.

If the concept for The Contemporary as I am describing it is sounding very 'BALTIC', it's because the model is not, in some ways, dissimilar, except that we didn't have a building. But the spirit, I think, was very close. We really wanted to press at the boundaries of both what was defining art at the time as well as what museums were doing in terms of exhibition-making; thinking in new ways about what it meant to actually curate. To that end, we showed a lot of art that I like to refer to as 'genre bending': art that really doesn't fit very easily into any categories at all.

On the cusp of a major professional transition, I find myself in the privileged position of being able to reflect on my four years in London, and also able to speak frankly about some of the things that have worked for me and some of the places where I think I've had glorious failures. But I first want to just show you a couple of projects organised by The Contemporary to give you a sense of my background. This was a project by the artist Alison Saar called 'Catfish Dreamin''. The Contemporary believed that a 'museum' is a state of mind and not a building. In fact, 'Catfish Dreamin'' was installed on the back of a 1959 Chevy pick-up truck. We just drove it into the parking lots of libraries, hospitals and schools, and even parked it on the Mall in Washington D.C. outside the Smithsonian Museums.

Before we could convince the city that we needed a museum for contemporary art, they asked us to go out and give the community a taste of its identity and what kinds of things it would do. Without a permanent site, and because there was only a limited audience for such a museum, we decided to create an audience by bringing exhibitions directly to communities. Since Baltimore is a city of neighbourhoods, this became a source of inspiration for us and for the artists with whom we worked. George is a Baltimore native, so he had a passionate commitment to making the museum accessible to everyone. We wanted to break down the barriers between artists and audiences, and the residencies really helped our community get over their initial hesitation that contemporary art had little to do with their lives, because when they interacted with the artists and participated in the creation of art or the development of public programmes, and even helped renovate buildings for exhibitions, it gave them a real investment in what we were doing. They were the fabric of the museum. The Contemporary represented the collective desire of the people who got involved, to bring art into their daily lives.

We also did a project with the British artist Paul Etienne Lincoln, who was recently shown in the UK at the Henry Moore Foundation. This work was installed amongst the flora and fauna of a Victorian greenhouse. Paul was inspired by the opera singer Rosa Ponsell, who made her home in Baltimore. She married the mayor's son after she retired from the Metropolitan Opera. His installation, 'Ignisfatuus', was a contraption linked by tubes to three bell jars containing resin casts of a heart, a brain and lungs cast from human cadavers. To facilitate the casts, The Contemporary collaborated with the Maryland State Anatomy Board. Most of our projects were inter-disciplinary and collaborative and involved working with non-art 'partners'. How did this object work? A gramophone that looked like a strange insect was fully loaded with recordings of Rosa Ponsell singing arias that related to nature. On the twenty-eighth day of the month, the gramophone would start playing, the sound would get increasingly louder and fluorescing liquid would flow through the tubes. Printed inside those tubes were the musical notations of the arias and they would get rinsed away by the invisible fluorescing liquid, and you would see the whole place glow Yves Klein blue from the outside of the greenhouse. It was quite spectacular.

Those are two shows we did that were not in museum environments. Two that were in museum environments involved the use of permanent collections. Perhaps the most well known example was Fred Wilson's 'Mining the Museum' (1992). It took place in a conservative historical society and was a project in which the artist got an opportunity to create an installation that looked like a museum exhibition. Fred is African-American and as he studied the collection he asked , 'Where am I reflected in this museum?' The opening gesture of his installation was a 'truth trophy' that was given (without irony) for truth in advertising! On either side of the trophy were busts of three white men such as Napoleon – who had nothing to do with Maryland history but whose effigies were in the collection – and three black historical figures, Benjamin Bannecker, Harriet Tubman and Frederick Douglass, who all lived in Maryland and had a huge impact on the state's history, but were not represented in the collection. This set the ball rolling to get you to begin to look at these objects through his eyes and to ask how museums make decisions about what to include and what to exclude; i.e. whose history is being told through a collection?

When the Serpentine called in 1997 and asked me to come for an interview, I had heard the hype about the London art scene. I was, of course, curious, but also a little wary. Working outside of a centre, in a place like Baltimore, had given me an enviable degree of creative freedom as you can see. While my colleagues in places like New York had to juggle all kinds of politics, The Contemporary was protected. We had no shortage of dialogue with our colleagues nationally. Curators and artists were always coming to Baltimore to check out what we were up to and we received reviews in The New York Times and the usual art world periodicals, and soon our colleagues were studying the model we had developed.

But even though The Contemporary was set up as a non-institution, one day I woke up and realised I had become formulaic. I thought, 'Wait a minute, if I'm going to continue to develop intellectually, I need to think about other kinds of exhibition-making.' I also needed to take on the challenge of being in a 'real' institution to see if some of my ideas about context, for example, were actually transferable.

The Serpentine programme includes historic figures such as Louise Bourgeois, Brice Marden, Yayoi Kusama and Bridget Riley. We have a very strong commitment to British artists: we've shown Gillian Wearing, Jane and Louise Wilson, Cornelia Parker and Chris Ofili, as well as international figures like Andreas Gursky, William Kentridge and Shirin Neshat. It's funny, when I was putting the slides together for this talk, I realised that in four years I had curated something like twenty exhibitions. I would not have been able to do it without the Serpentine team. It is extraordinary what this team accomplishes and it is a team ethic that enables us to be extremely light on our feet.

Perhaps one of the biggest challenges for me working at the Serpentine has been the building itself: it is isolated in Kensington Gardens and sometimes I feel cut off from reality. It is in the middle of a city but feels like it is in Arcadia. But I think that is why it can do such a challenging programme. Visitors are very open by the time they walk through the park, take in the fountains and foliage and are then confronted by something unfamiliar and challenging. At first I was very resistant to the gem-like quality of the perfectly symmetrical architecture. It took time to figure out how to use it to the advantage of the works of art and also how and when to resist it and to play with its context. I know that this is a priority for our director and she is working with Doug Aitken on a project for Fall 2001 that will really turn the space on its ear ('New Ocean', Oct-Nov 2001).

The Mariko Mori (1998) exhibition was the first in which I began to explore the building, although I should say that in exhibitions like the Richard Wilson project before the renovation, to site just one example, this had already been done. We placed a Himowari device, this being an instrument for filtering ultra-violet light out of the sunrays in order to provide pure sunlight, on the roof of the gallery. (The artist's father invented this machine.) By means of a fibre-optic cable, the Himowari device illuminated Mariko's sculpture, 'Enlightenment Capsule', inside the gallery. This work really came alive when the sunlight hit the multi-coloured lotus blossom inside the 'Capsule', and refracted, spilling light over the plinth, which was about three metres in diameter. Mariko's 3-D video, 'Nirvana', was placed in a neighbouring space. Both works, though technically very different, inspired the same sense of wonder.

For me, one of the high points of my tenure at the Serpentine was the exhibition of the work of Felix Gonzales-Torres (2000), an artist who had a huge impact on me as a curator. I wanted to focus on how this artist explored context. His work was so much about accessibility and about turning the audience into an active generator of meaning. We expanded our walls by placing his works in sites throughout the city. 'America', his only outdoor light piece, was produced in collaboration with Camden Arts Centre; there was a billboard project across London and another light piece in a local hospital. Students from the Royal College of Art showed the artist's jigsaws in their studios and the public had to see them by visiting the student artists and talking to them about Felix's work. The public could also request his jigsaws at the V&A in the Department of Drawings, Prints and Photographs.

When Ralph Rugoff and I co-curated 'The Greenhouse Effect' (2000), we wanted to remind people that a park is a manicured and artificially constructed landscape. When they looked through the window of the gallery, we hoped that Kensington Gardens would look more 'artful' than the exhibited works of art. The exhibition presented objects that were alive and some that only appeared to be alive. Tim Hawkinson made a tiny little bird out of his fingernail clippings ('Bird', 1997) and many younger visitors were convinced that this was a specimen bird's skeleton, in the same way that they thought Anya Gallaccio's apple tree ('Untitled', 2000) could not possibly be real because 'trees don't get put inside museums'. A remarkable piece by Rachel Berwick ('May-por-é', 1998) consisted of an aviary housing two live parrots, but Roxy Paine's mushrooms that looked like they were colonising the gallery floor, were actually synthetic ('Psilocybe Cubensis Field', 1997). Henrik Håkansson took on the subject of 'the wildlife garden', that of course was not wild at all, outside the Natural History Museum on Cromwell Road. He created a surveillance system ('10 seconds of forever (today)', 2000) that channelled video images onto a screen installed alongside an African safari diorama inside the museum. Visitors could watch frogs spawning and birds nesting as nature was mediated via the cameras that Henrik had planted around the museum's garden. This was the closest to live nature that they would find in a museum of dead nature.

'Give & Take', a collaboration with the V & A (January – April 2001), continued our work with colleague institutions in South Kensington. For this two-site exhibition, the Serpentine invited Hans Haacke to do an installation at the gallery. The artist selected one hundred and eighty objects from the V & A's collections. Unlike museum critiques such as the Fred Wilson project, Haacke demonstrated that it is not only museums that send mixed messages, but also the objects themselves. The show at the V & A presents the work of fifteen contemporary artists, juxta-posed with works in the Museum's collection. A banner by Xu Bing, 'Art for the People', written in Chinglish, a language invented by the artist, which looks like Chinese letters but is actually is made up of English letters painted in faux Chinese calligraphy; a photograph by Hiroshi Sugimoto of a Queen Victoria waxwork, taken at Madame Tussaud's, hangs where a patron portrait would in the V & A; an installation of eight sculptures by Marc Quinn is juxtaposed with the neo-classical sculpture collection. Marc's sculptures depict disabled people who were either born with limbs missing, or who lost them through illness or accident, in white Macedonian marble, with no veining, so they look really artificial. Photographs by Andres Serrano of religious themes, or which use symbolism that very strongly relates to Christian iconography, appear alongside medieval Christian objects. 'Precious Blood', for example, which depicts the artist's blood and urine, is seen in the vicinity of jewel encrusted chalices and reliquaries. Roxy Paine's 'Scumak' is displayed with the 'Fakes and Forgeries' collection. It (the work) actually produces sculptures. You should know that the V & A, at one time, was a museum of manufacturing, so it would not have been unusual to see machinery like this in its halls in the nineteenth century.

I wanted to say something about my new post at the Seattle Art Museum and my decision to go to this particular museum. I realised that, as in the case of The Contemporary, there is the real possibility of my becoming formulaic again. I increasingly feel myself drawn back to working with historical collections, and at the same time, monographic exhibitions are beginning to feel limited. For the first time I will be working with a general collection. I am responsible, with a team of curators, for objects that start with Ancient Egypt and come all the way to the present, with great strengths in African and Asian art. Many important collections of modern and contemporary art have also been promised to the museum and when the holdings are increased through the addition of these collections, it will be, arguably, one of the premiere West Coast institutions.

The Seattle Art Museum has three sites: an Asian Art Museum, which is one of the finest in America, a downtown museum designed by Robert Venturi surveying the entire collection including modern and contemporary art, and the new Olympic Sculpture Park which will be completed in 2004. The Park will be an evolving public space where art can happen. There will be publicly sited works of art, but not all of them will be permanent. It will also be a centre for discussion on publicly sited art as well as broader issues related to culture and cities.

I decided to go Seattle because I had to stop playing with everybody else's toys and take on some of the very difficult issues that having a collection of that kind of scope really poses. When the recent earthquake struck Seattle, I quickly called the museum and said, 'Do I even have a museum to come to anymore?' They said, 'Everything's fine. Only one object was damaged.' I was always so preoccupied with the creative re-installation of collections that I realised the time had come to absorb the fact that there are practical realities that I am going to have to deal with for the first time on a daily basis; i.e. that every single object in the museum has to be on a special kind of plinth that can resist earthquakes, meaning that every time you move an object, both the cost and the time implications are considerable.

I am now adjusting to the fact that I am working in a repository of cultural artefacts and cultural values. I'm interested, as when I came to the Serpentine, to find out what that place will make of me and what I will make of them and how I will change one more time as a curator. I think it is important to constantly re-invent yourself in this profession, to stir things up. So I'm getting ready to shed another skin and to see what develops.

(Audience applause)

JON BEWLEY:

My name is Jon Bewley and I run an organisation called
Locus+ with Simon Herbert. I'd like to thank the BALTIC
and the University for inviting me to show you some slides
today, and I really enjoyed Lisa's talk.

I'm going to talk a little bit about myself and how I got
into organising artists' events, and then I'm going to
concentrate on talking about just four of the many projects
that we've organised over the last eight years. I hope that
by describing them quite briefly, you'll get a sense of what
Simon and I are interested in, in terms of working with
artists, what our sensibilities are and the kind of things
that we're committed to in terms of methodology and
attitude.

I'm actually from the region, and I came to Newcastle
over twenty years ago to study on the Fine Art BA at
Newcastle Polytechnic. During my second year in the new
media department, it became apparent that I couldn't
actually show the kind of artworks that I was making
within the department for various practical and technical
reasons. It wasn't just me who was having that feeling of
rubbing up against the institution. One of the others was
Richard Grayson, who I understand gave a talk here last
week, which I unfortunately missed. He was also an
undergraduate with me.

As undergraduates, in order to find a situation in which
we could satisfy that need to make the kind of things that
we wanted to, a small group of us got together and ran a
collective in Newcastle called The Basement Group – so-
called because it was physically based in a warehouse
basement. The group purposefully constituted itself as a
collective and we shared responsibilities. We operated an
open access policy, in terms of, 'there's space for everybody', and we ran it on quite open lines. The space itself
was simply a concrete room, which was able to accom-
modate a variety of principally time-based events: performance, installation, video screenings, etc. Events were

programmed every Wednesday and Saturday, and ranged from short monologues through to durational works lasting a number of days. The focus was principally on conceptual and process-based works: non-narrative in nature and particularly prevalent at that time as part of an alternative non-institutional art scene.

In addition to inviting more people to Newcastle to show in The Basement, we were already administering other exhibitions and events. As The Basement got known, artists said, 'You've got these resources? Do we have to do something at The Basement? Can't we do something elsewhere?'

So in 1984 we decided to retire The Basement, after six years and more than 230 events, in favour of establishing an organisation that was only office-based. We decided we would pursue, if we could raise funds, a strategy where we would have resources that were geared to introducing works into an arena where context or the site where they were presented was an essential part of how the works were read. That organisation was called Projects UK. There was an overlap between The Basement and Projects UK as the former declined and the latter was established. Projects UK was the first office-based outfit in this country, modelled on and informed, in part, by the attitude of a European organisation in Amsterdam called De Appel and Art Metropol in Toronto, Canada, both of which had galleries but had a different sensibility. Basically, we discarded the bricks and mortar. Throughout the eighties we presented events in Newcastle and in the surrounding region. Unlike the first-come-first-served policy adopted by The Basement, Projects UK enforced a curatorial filter, for two main reasons. Firstly, we did not have the resources – either in terms of finance, personnel or whatever – to realise every proposal made to us, now that we were operating out of the controlled environment of The Basement. Secondly, we also wanted to be able to initiate certain projects rather than just respond to whatever came through the post. Projects UK ran until 1992, but I left in 1990, when I was involved in curating large festivals of site-specific temporary work for an organisation called the Edge Biennale Trust, an experience which, although interesting and exciting, wasn't very satisfactory. We were herding huge numbers of artists into warehouses in Newcastle and Madrid and London, and having great parties, but it wasn't very interesting intellectually for me.

In 1992 I returned to Newcastle and was involved in writing or feeding ideas into documents for a bid for the region to host the Year of Visual Artists and other lottery bids. Simon Herbert and I met up again, and by now Projects UK had also closed, so we decided to set up this organisation called Locus+. In terms of the history of having worked with an artists' collective, and then through Projects UK working with artists, this next stage posed an interesting question: if there was going to be another organisation, I had to figure out where it was going to go, what gap it was going to fit, why I was interested in doing it and how was the world changing?

So the organisation – again it's office-based – is called Locus+. It was conceived not to have a title, it was conceived to be a graphic, which would be a circle with the 'L' and a cross in it. It's called Locus+ because a locus is a fixed point; it's not an arbitrary point, it's where three lines cross in mathematics. Obviously that locus, that place, that site, can be anything: geographical, political, social, whatever. People imagine the '+' is about artists, and that's fine. But actually the '+' is not just artists, it's the conjunction of artists with others. All the projects that we do involve collaborative works with different kinds of institutions and systems to bring them into the world. For instance, we have collaborated with non-art bodies ranging from the police and fire services through to community writing groups and the International Association of Lighthouse Authorities. Each individual project tends, overall, to be completely different and adds a different dynamic to our programme shape.

I can't believe I've condensed so much history into about four minutes! No doubt I've left something out. The important thing to take from this extremely expurgated version is the manifest attempt to adapt the organisational strategy over time, both in order to respond to the changing cultural landscape but also, hopefully, to initiate and create new opportunities for artists and audiences.

I'll describe these four projects in terms of how they came into being. I've picked each of these projects because they illustrate a particular method of working with artists. Some of them came out of the blue and we didn't expect them; some were opportunities which you might not think that an organisation like Locus+ would take. They illustrate differing scales and ideas of what site-specific art could be. We've produced approximately forty projects since 1993. In addition, we also maintain a publishing strategy, which so far has resulted in more than twenty-five catalogues and artists' multiples. We also have an archive currently being developed for public access at the University of Sunderland: a massive resource of over 12,000 images and 150 hours of video tape, which principally documents our projects since 1978.

(Slides) Stefan Gec's 'Buoy', premiered at the Maritime Museum, Hartlepool, in 1996, was a project that was actually begun over ten years earlier. We have worked on a number of different projects with Stefan – both as Projects UK and Locus+ – but 'Buoy' is a project that spans both organisations. Stefan is an artist who also studied at Newcastle. He's a second generation Ukrainian – his father was a refugee – and he uses his personal history as a place in the metaphorical values of the work that he makes. It's very autobiographical in a sense that's quite discreet, but it's also quite expansive, in a funny sort of way.

The precursor to 'Buoy' was 'Trace Elements' (1989), which was part of a national sculpture project called 'TSWA' that Projects UK was acting as northern curator/producer for. Stefan had identified eight Soviet Whisky Class submarines that were being scrapped in a decommissioning shipyard in Blyth (about 40 miles up the coast from Newcastle) as part of the detente process of that time, at the end of the Cold War. His proposal was that he would like to take a section of steel from each submarine and re-cast the metal into a public sculpture: a set of eight bells. These bells were then suspended from a pontoon on the High Level Bridge (in Newcastle) on what is called the littoral: the mid-point between high and low tides. On one hand, 'Trace Elements' hinted at a concept of swords into ploughshares – that these instruments of war had been metamorphosed into instruments of celebration or warning – but also these new versions still mimicked their source, as they disappeared beneath the current at high tide.

When originally conceived by Stefan, it was always intended that the bells would be re-transformed into something else again in the future: they would come down at the end of that finite project and at a later date, would become a boat or something else, and would then have another life. In fact, what happened in 1996 was that Locus+ and Stefan had the bells re-melted down, and they were used in the construction of a fully operational Class IV Marker ocean-going replacement buoy (which is why the colour is yellow and black). We liaised with the International Association of Lighthouse Authorities, based in Paris – the body responsible for organising the movement of marker buoys in the non-territorial waters in the North Atlantic – and donated the buoy to them as a working object. It is on the high seas now. The IALA will take it out, if there's a damaged deep-sea marker, and replace it with Stefan's buoy while the original marker is being repaired. Over a period of years, if you had a series of charts, the location of the buoy would mark, in reverse, the original route that the Soviet submarines took coming out of the Baltic to go into the North Atlantic during the Cold War.

There's a supplementary dynamic to this: the blue box on the top is solar panelling and the buoy is what's known as a 'smart buoy'; that is, every twelve hours it transmits data back to a website on the physical state of the sea around it. So you could visit it if you desired, and you could find out about the temperature, the hours of sunlight, salinity, swell, wind direction and so on. So it is in the world and it is about exactly where it is. But it's somewhere on the high seas doing a job.

'Fairy Tales and Factories' (1999) was a temporary installation work made by Laura Vickerson, who is Canadian and lives in Calgary. I had met Laura on a studio visit and liked very much what she made, which was sculpture using organic materials, and – as is often the case when we visit artists – I asked her to keep us informed about her practice, with a view to doing something down the line. Not long after, she contacted Locus+ and said, 'I'd like to do a project in a textile mill.' So we said that we would try to figure it out and, eventually, with the help of many people, we found Farfield Mill in Sedburgh, a small village of about seven hundred souls in Cumbria. The mill had closed in 1992 after being a fully working mill for a hundred and thirty-odd years.

For this project, we put together a coalition of paid helpers – a group of female art students from the University (of Newcastle) – to construct a sculpture by pinning individual rose petals together. The advance work took place over four months, with the students pinning over 700,000 rose petals to a muslin train. The final part of the train was completed in the two weeks immediately prior to the exhibition by a group of women based locally in Sedburgh called the Sedburgh Stitchers, who used to work in the factory.

The mill itself was in a state of extensive chaos and dilapidation. The exhibition space was in the roof of the mill, which we cleared out while the Sedburgh Stitchers worked on the train on the ground floor. Laura's artwork eventually took the form of a 30 metre long garment that ran the length of the mill floor. As the title indicated, it was simultaneously mystical or magical, but also the result of repetitive and mundane industry. There were yellow rose petals inside the hood.

The artwork itself was only exhibited for two days, which may seem a relatively short period of time given the months it took to make the work, but this was also part of a calculated strategy to have the localised context decide aspects of its presentation; specifically, that the work was premiered for the duration of the local spring fair, which lasted two days. There was an intense response in terms of audience and the people who came to visit. The object itself and the stories about it being made were all in the countryside and it's ownership was very much of the place and the people who were in it. People came back to the factory who used to work there: I met people who had spent fifty years working in this factory and they'd come back and there was this extraordinary object that had been put into it. So I've got a 'who and what is the audience?' subtext going with some of these projects.

The other two projects that I am going to describe happened at the same time and were specifically commissioned as existing in close physical proximity to one another. We were approached by the owner of Compton Verney, a private estate, owned by Peter Moores of Littlewoods fame and fortune. It's a seventeenth-century Robert Adam house in a Capability Brown landscape; extraordinarily beautiful. He's having it refurbished to house his art collection of mainly eighteenth-century Italian portraiture. Both the house and grounds are currently closed during the renovation, but the grounds are opened to the public during the summer as part of an advance public awareness strategy called 'Art in the Park'. Different individuals/organisations are invited each year to make a curatorial proposal and Richard Grey, the Director at Compton Verney, approached Simon and I in 2000. We said that we would consider it, but that there were certain conditions that would have to apply: that we would pick artists that we wanted to work with (we don't project manage other people's projects). They were very good about it and said, 'Yes, ok.' We spent a few weeks there and we were talking to various people: people in the village and people who used to work in the house. We collated a file of historical information and then we asked two artists to make proposals. One was Simon Patterson and the other was Anya Gallacio. We hadn't worked with Simon before, but again we had been in contact with him over a period of time, waiting to see if the conditions would come together for something to happen. With Anya, we had as previously commissioned a large temporary public artwork as part of Artranspennine98.

The two projects had to run at the same time and it was going to be interesting to see how the artists would solve the problem of being in this physical landscape and making new works, and whether they were interested in doing it, which they both were. Simon's piece was based on two historical facts that he'd discovered. One was that when the building was opened, they used to have large floating tableaux on the lake that involved pyrotechnics, smoke and fireworks, etc. Also, during the Second World War, the War Ministry had taken control of the grounds at Compton Verney Estate in order to test smoke conceal-ment devices for troops in battle. There's also another personal thing that Simon found out: during the Second World War we had a thing here called the Invisible Army, which was people who were infirm or too old to fight, but who used to wear uniforms and move around the country, to give people the impression we had far more soldiers than we actually had. Simon's grandfather was in the

Invisible Army and was actually stationed at Compton Verney during the Second World War – it was just a fluke.

Anyway, Simon's idea also related to the sublime Capability Brown landscape and the fact that there are key points where you can see it from. He conflated the two historical things in terms of colour and spectacle, siting a number of different smoke emission devices around these key points that would set off different colours of smoke at different times of the day in a co-ordinated way. To see all of them, you had to move around the grounds and the house in order to catch them. There were five different colours – red, yellow, blue, green, white – and they all had different military values. They would kind of 'happen': if it was very still they would linger in the air and if it was very windy they would just disappear. So that was a kind of performative, theatrical thing for the landscape.

The second piece was Anya Gallacio, who makes work in organic materials which over a period of time transform themselves: they disappear or mutate; the mutability is made visible. She also started digging around in the filing cabinets in the V & A, and came across a Robert Adam motif that was designed for the ceiling of the Great House but was never implemented. She said, 'What I'd like to do is to somehow instigate this motif into the landscape.' With the aid of chartered surveyors and a huge team of people, we had templates made and pegged out in the gardens. We cut away tonnes of grass and the shape of the Adam motif slowly appeared. The estate manager allowed us to grow the grass back and eventually the motif just faded away.

(Audience applause)

ANDY THOMSON:

I suppose the thing to do in terms of the discussion is to pick up on a couple of points. I think that these two projects represent a synergy really, because they have parallels but don't cross over with one another that much. However they do both have an interest in site-specificity. I think it would be interesting to see what you both thought about one another's projects or curatorial direction, and the import you think you might be having in terms of the art world? I think that, obviously, curators have an idea about their direction and the things they would like to present to the public. But I have often wondered, and asked curators, how they have made their decisions about which artists they use and the way exhibition programmes are created and constructed. Of the curators I have asked in Australia, the more frank ones have said that it all depends on what they saw in art magazines, art fairs, recent local and international exhibitions. Others have said that it had a more theoretical basis. Could we approach it from this angle to start with, and look at the site-specific art in your presentations, a focus that comes out of, dare I say, a postmodern project? Can I ask you first Lisa?

LISA CORRIN:

I would just want to expand the term 'site specific' to say 'context specific'. Most curators come into a new position with a checklist of shows that they want to do. I no longer feel that this is entirely appropriate. After my experience at the Serpentine, I tend to think it is better to start with the realisation that one doesn't know a place. I am not catholic in my taste in contemporary art. I hope that the programme that Julia (Peyton-Jones) and I have developed together has been diverse. But I do feel the need to immerse myself in the sensibility of London or Seattle or wherever, to absorb the quality of a museum's spaces, to get a sense of what artists are doing and what kinds of work we could present that would feed the dialogue that is happening in studios. There was also, in the case of the Serpentine, a concern that certain artists like Felix (Gonzales-Torres) had never been seen in-depth in this country and so I felt that we had an obligation to redress the balance historically. Once I get acclimatised, certain things just jump out at me. I felt, for example, that Felix's work, like Dan Flavin's, would look spectacular in the Serpentine's spaces and play on its strengths and special qualities.

'The Greenhouse Effect' (2000) came out of a dialogue between Ralph (Rugoff) and I: we were talking about the relationship between the park and the building. I had kept a file for almost ten years of artists that worked with living things. Ralph also wanted the chaos of nature to encroach upon the pristine quality of the gallery spaces. The fact that the Serpentine is located on Exhibition Road also led me to propose to my director the series of projects which would link all the different institutions in South Kensington to the Serpentine (such as 'Give & Take'), and us to them, in a really profound way. This was the kind of collaborative work I had done in Baltimore. I think the challenge for a curator with an institution that has to programme in a gallery, is not only the commissioning of site-specific works such as doing projects all over the city like Artangel, but also how to make the permanent gallery spaces constantly feel different each time an exhibition is presented. A lot of people have commented that the Serpentine seems utterly transformed from project to project. Our gallery manager Mike Gaughan is a master at this game. I think that during 'The Greenhouse Effect' the inside of the building really did feel magical and as though it was alive. We have to make our walls porous, so that we're not limited by the gallery spaces.

ANDY THOMSON (TO JON BEWLEY):

Do you have the same kinds of ideas, about site-specificity?

JON BEWLEY:

Well, first of all I'd say that I don't consider myself to be a curator, although from the outside it probably looks as though I am. In terms of having fifteen minutes to try to give a shape to some of the things that Simon and I have done, it's a difficult editing process that I've had to do this afternoon; trying to judge who was going to be here and what have you. Because this idea of site or situation, the conflict or the crisis of the white box, is not in our office. So, we have done these theatrical, outdoor things and we're working with artists at completely different levels of their careers, from very recent graduates to people who are relatively well known. The actual format of how anything is manifest in the world is not prescribed. It could be a TV broadcast, which we did with Wendy Kirkup and Pat Naldi in the first Locus+ project ('Search', 1993), or a performance/video/broadcast work. We do videos, we do CD's, we do books, we do multiples. Locus+ is really about creating opportunities for artists to move into new formats or into a new situation. That situation could be anything.

ANDY THOMSON:

So if you're not a curator, you're a commissioner? How would you describe your role?

JON BEWLEY:

It all depends how you define the word 'curator'. If you have somebody who orders groups of things in some way and mediates them into the world, if that's the definition of a curator, I would say that I'd be a curator. But my relationship with working with artists is that artists tend to come to us as opposed to us going out into the world and choosing them and then herding them together, which is one of the reasons I found the festival format of time-based stuff unproductive. So, I've kind of got a really great situation, because artists come to us and say, 'Would you be interested in doing this?' or 'Do you think you could do that?' Your supplementary was how do you decide which projects to do? That's a question that always comes up: who takes responsibility for it? I do! The reason why you make the decision is that every single project is different: can you raise the money? Is it technically feasible? Do Simon and I actually want to spend eight months of our lives fundraising and then putting our heads above the parapet if we don't believe in that project? And believe in it how? One of functions and one of the things we believe in, is the value of artists working in the real world, working with real people in real systems, and taking certain things into the world that we think are of value and important to the way people live. That's how I want to live my life. It's an important thing. Visual arts have value in a way that can impact positively on the way in which people ask questions of each other. Those questions can be really difficult and we've done projects that are difficult.

ANDY THOMSON:

You mean they're difficult for the public?

JON BEWLEY:

The content is difficult. We did a project of Shane Cullen paintings inside the Irish Centre in Newcastle ('Fragmens sur les Institutions Républicaines IV', 1996). Large text paintings of the diaries of Irish hunger strikers. Politically, it could be quite difficult. But those projects that ask questions about the role of artists primarily, but also about how you understand art, are the interesting questions.

Because what you have then are different groups asking different questions of each other. There's a discourse.

ANDY THOMSON:

Talking of discourse, does anybody want to field a question in this context?

QUESTION:

You mentioned the word 'freedom' a couple of times earlier on; that you were looking for freedom as a curator. Freedom is something that perhaps one associates more with an artist, a creative person. I began to wonder, in the same way that painters are sometimes accused of being frustrated sculptors, whether curators are perhaps frustrated artists?

LISA CORRIN:

I'm not a frustrated artist! I never wanted to be an artist, never studied art; in fact, I started out as an historian. One of the things that interests me is the whole notion of time. You take chronology out of the museum and where do you wind up? I am thinking about what it means to be a 'contemporaneous museum'. That it to say, not a museum of contemporary art, but a museum of changing perspectives. The contemporaneous museum is an institution within an institution, where you have someone who's really there as a catalyst, not only to raise questions about the collection, but also to create exhibitions and dialogues that force the museum to constantly re-think its perspective. So it's a bit like the Office of Frames – try to imagine this – where you might have one or two people and all there is, is a box of frames. They walk around the museum all the time holding the frames up in front of the other framed or vitrined objects, forcing you to see them this way or this way, so that what is on view is constantly being re-interpreted. At the same time, curators, who are the specialists, are also forced to look through lots of different frames. Think of it as the silent intellectual conscience of the museum. In a way, 'Give & Take', the collaboration with the V & A, was an attempt to do that. It wasn't merely some coy intervention or critique of the V & A. In fact, it's outside of that genre altogether. What I kept telling my colleagues there was that this is a project that shows you what really is possible. There's nothing that says that Andres Serrano cannot be in the medieval treasury of the V & A anytime we want him to be. The only thing that keeps them from being there is the system, which is like the 40, 000lb gorilla that's been in place for a hundred and fifty years and no one is willing to move. Actually, the thing that limits curators most is their own lack of imagination. The curatorial team in Seattle is looking forward to exploring a new conceptual model within which an encyclopaedic-type museum can function.

COMMENT FROM AUDIENCE:

I was a little bit provoked by the way you both translated your projects. Forgive me for saying this critically, but I think of both of you as people who've made all sorts of quite tough projects, but that somehow didn't come across in your talks. A lot of the things that you've both done have been very uncomfortable, even disliked and quite contentious, political, in a way. Neither of you talked about that.

LISA CORRIN:

I'll talk about that! (Audience laughter)

QUESTION:

For example, John, how much continuity is there between the early Projects UK things and what you're doing now?

It seems like a big shift of direction. And Lisa, you spoke about the first show you did at the Serpentine ('Loose Threads') as being pretty unsatisfactory. At the same time, it was probably the most radical show you did there. There seems to be a reluctance on both your parts to analyse or discuss any of this.

LISA CORRIN:

I'm happy to talk about politics! Thank you for asking that question because it's hard in twenty minutes to do more than give an overview. But I think you're absolutely right. I can tell you that working on that V & A project was no party. Hans Haacke's work, I think, is well known to the people in this room. So you know the issues that he deals with, you know his history with the media and the museum community. Part of the Serpentine's role was to insist upon a no censorship agreement. Then to take curators, heads of departments, distinguished and eminent scholars, who have a vested interest in the way their collections are presented, and convince them that putting Andres Serrano with the mediaeval treasury, is actually a very good idea. Similarly, working with conservators at the V & A to convince them that objects that the V & A doesn't even allow their own curators to move, should move across the street to the Serpentine Gallery. It was one the most difficult projects of my career, the entire Serpentine team had a lot of sleepless nights, but it pulled us together and demonstrated what is possible. It had the same impact at the V&A I think, too. We were exhausted but exhilarated, or at least I was. Ironically, this project, without question, catalysed my departure from the Serpentine in so far as I realised that museums can change, even museums like the V&A that seem so fraught and entrenched. But truth be told, and it may sound hyperbolic, I really want to change the world, to get people to think critically so they can make informed decisions about their lives and I think museums can contribute to this. I decided that if I really wanted to change the world, or at least the world inside the museum, I had to be in a leadership position, to captain an unwieldy ship, which is what big collecting institutions often are, I am afraid. This seemed so worthwhile given the potential results. There is nothing that heartens me more than when someone leaves an exhibition with which I have been affiliated and they tell me that the experience has altered their view of the world or that they don't entirely understand what they have seen, but that it has given them food for thought. I am even pleased when they say they don't like it, because through their experience of visiting the museum they have developed a vocabulary that enables them to articulate an opinion and the confidence to express it. I think if one is going to curate, he or she must be prepared to take on tough issues, to have a thick skin. As for me, I don't think it's worth doing if it's easy.

JON BEWLEY (TO QUESTIONER):

Is that what you meant?

QUESTION:

What did you think I meant?

JON BEWLEY:

Afterwards I'd like you to tell me all the projects we did that were so disliked.

QUESTION:

I don't mean 'disliked' in a negative way...

JON BEWLEY:

They were uncomfortable, I know. What I wanted to say about that was that we don't actually think that any of our projects are difficult to do. I mean, it's not easy to put seventy tonne columns of salt in the river (referring to 'Two Sisters', 1998) in terms of the systems in the world. We needed to get different licenses and permissions. But the process of delivering a project as complicated and as difficult as that is to a certain extent also part of that work. Because we have to go to people and sit in offices, with a marine engineer, or a chartered surveyor or whatever, to help us to realise it. And then we have to make the case that it's worthwhile them getting involved. Because a lot of people who help us do the projects, they might get paid initially, but then suddenly you tap into an energy, so that people want to get involved and they contribute much more than you expect and assist in the delivery. So my point is, that process of bringing lots of different people on board is also part of revealing the systems that make those works exist. I'm not just talking to engineers here; I'm talking to the committee of the Irish Centre, chaired by a priest, looking at documentation of the Shane Cullen things and then talking to the city planning officer in Hull about getting permission to move things around on the river, etc.

QUESTION:

One of the things that you said, which I thought was really important, was that the selection of works was on the basis of belief, belief in the projects. So I'm really asking, what do you believe in? If it doesn't cause some kind of premature foreclosure, I'd like to ask you how you describe your agenda or your project as it's evolved over a period of time?

JON BEWLEY:

It seems to me there has to be a role of advocacy, through an organisation like Locus+ say, but through many organisations that advocate positive places for artists in the world. That's one of the things that I believe in: trying to create a situation where that happens. Making life difficult for artists as well as the people they engage with and the reasons they are doing what they do. If you wanted to know what my value system is and how it's reflected, the different facets of it through working with artists, then buy this book! (Holds up copy of 'Locus Solus: site, identity, technology in contemporary art', Black Dog Publishing, London, 2000.) (Audience laughter)

LISA CORRIN:

I'd like to add something to this. I want to go on record saying what I believe. I am a feminist. In the way some people might say, 'I am a Jew' or 'I am a Catholic', I am a feminist and I say that proudly. What that means to me is that in all of the work that I do, the choices I make and the artists whom I show – and that doesn't mean just showing women artists – I ask questions about who's been left out. What other ways of thinking need to be represented? I look at work very closely in terms of the questions it raises about the things we would prefer not to discuss in polite company, like race, sexuality, religion: anything that has to do with identity as a complex structure. I am deeply committed to exactly what Jon just said about projects that give us an opportunity to reveal the institutional biases and infrastructures that invisibly work within our society and frame the way we think and behave.

I also believe that all forms of creativity have a right to be represented. When Julia (Peyton-Jones) and I work on the Serpentine's programme, we literally do what we call 'the Chinese menu approach' to the schedule: we choose one from column A, one from column B. Is there video on the programme? Is there photography? Is there sculpture? Are women being represented? Are people of colour being represented? Are artists at different points in their career being represented? One thing I could be faulted for is having a higher percentage of Americans on the menu than perhaps some people might like, because I am an American and you know, you show what you know. That's what I know best and as I've learned about other things, they've come into the programme too. But this has been a learning experience for me because I was as provincial as any curator having an East Coast American mentality. And part of the reason for coming here was to open out onto another territory.

ANDY THOMSON:

It's a bit hard to follow that...

JON BEWLEY:

I subscribe to all that as well!

ANDY THOMSON:

Would you say that Jon? Maybe you perceived yourself in some different position to Lisa as far as the presentation of contemporary art was concerned? You don't work for an institution; Locus+ is your institution, one that you invented.

JON BEWLEY:

In a way we invented it out of fifteen years of other things. It didn't come out of nowhere; it came out of a mixture of personal histories and it also reflects the way artists work. Stefan's project, the buoy project, wasn't constructed for us. We're shaped around what artists do.

ANDY THOMSON:

But does the idea of Locus+, or some of the earlier ideas that you were involved with, come out of a reaction to the institution, or are they simply an attempt to find an alternative to ordinary institutional methods that artists might be compelled to make in order to present themselves?

JON BEWLEY:

I certainly don't think it's oppositional. It's not purposefully oppositional anyway.

ANDY THOMSON:

It's also at some point been focused in the North East?

JON BEWLEY:

Yes. I don't know if Richard (Grayson) touched on this at all last week, but it's not an accident that we are here. We came here as students and then we decided to stay. We've never done a project in London and we never will. Well, I should never say never. It's just that we are a long way away and we try to stay a long away, to stay here. In this country, the way in which cultural practice by artists is perceived, is dreadfully distorted by the centre because it's the media centre, the financial centre, the so-called cultural centre. The gradient is so steep that we wanted to see if we could create an opportunity device away from there. In it's little way I think that with that investment and the commitment we've had from artists, we've created something that's of itself, in another place. We often talk about this idea of the North East being a gateway or a doorway, where people weren't coming through London but they were coming into the situation through a different doorway, and we wanted that doorway to be in the North of England.

ANDY THOMSON:

It's great too because it means that international artists are coming through a different doorway, through your later projects.

JON BEWLEY:

And artists from here going out, which is pretty important.

LISA CORRIN:

This is an important issue and I'm really glad you just said that, because one of the challenges I'm facing in Seattle is they used to have a curator of North West regional art. The first question I was asked by the press was, not surprisingly, 'So, how are you going to make a contribution to regional art?' First of all, I don't believe in this term 'regional art'. There are artists who work in different places. My role as a curator is sometimes to show their work, but always to advocate. That is to say, to make my colleagues who haven't passed through our gateway, aware of the important work being done by the artists who live and work in my community so that they can take their place among their peers internationally. I challenge you to answer this question: 'what does an artist gain by being called a 'young British artist', a 'Newcastle artist'? It's important that the community is aware of the artists that live and work in any place. It's what keeps our communities alive and vibrant. But it's also important that the work of those artists is appreciated outside of their community so that they can have a dialogue and participate in the shaping of an international view of what constitutes contemporary ideas within contemporary culture.

ANDY THOMSON:

I think on that point we can wind up this very interesting discussion and I'd like to say thank you very much to both Lisa and Jon, and thank you all for coming.

(Audience applause)

SPEAKERS' BIOGRAPHIES

JON BEWLEY

Jon Bewley is a co-director (with Simon Herbert) of the
visual arts commissioning agency Locus+. One of the
foremost public art agencies in the UK, Locus+ has been
initiating projects with artists, primarily in non-gallery
locations, since 1993. An artist-run initiative that grew out
of two earlier organisations dedicated to time-based work
(The Basement Group, 1979-83 and Projects UK, 1983-
92), Locus+ works with artists on the production and
presentation of socially-engaged, collaborative and temporary projects. To date, they have completed over forty
projects with artists including Mark Wallinger ('A Real
Work of Art', 1994); Stefan Gec ('Trace Elements', 1990,
Detached Bell Tower, 1996 and Buoy, 1996); Anya
Gallacio ('Two Sisters', 1998 and 'Repens', 2000) and
Wendy Kirkup (Echo, 2000).

ANDREW BURTON

Andrew Burton is head of the Department of Fine Art and
Lecturer in Sculpture at the University of Newcastle. He is
a sculptor who has produced a number of major public
commissions including 'Annunciation', commissioned by
Sculpture at Goodwood (2000) and 'Cycle', commis-
sioned by Dudley Metropolitan Borough Council (2001).
He has had solo exhibitions at venues including the
Herbert Gallery, Coventry (2000) and the European
Ceramics Work Centre in the Netherlands (1996).

LISA CORRIN

Lisa Corrin was recently appointed Deputy Director for Art
/ Jon and Mary Shirley Curator of Modern and
Contemporary Art at the Seattle Art Museum. Prior to this,
she worked as chief curator at the Serpentine Gallery,

London (1997–2001). At the Serpentine, she curated numerous one-person shows including Brice Marden, Chris Ofili, Andreas Gursky, Bridget Riley and Felix Gonzales-Torres and group shows including 'Loose Threads' and (with Ralph Rugoff) 'The Greenhouse Effect'. More recently, she curated 'Give and Take', a two-site exhibition organised in collaboration with the Victoria and Albert Museum and the artist Hans Haacke (January – April 2001). From 1990-97 she served as chief curator of The Contemporary in Baltimore where she curated 'Mining the Museum', an installation by the African-American artist Fred Wilson and the Maryland Historical Society, and won the Wittenborn Prize for the accompanying publication. She is also co-author of a monograph on the artist Mark Dion published by Phaidon Press (1997).

RICHARD GRAYSON

Richard Grayson is Director of the Biennale of Sydney 2002. An artist, writer and curator who divides his time between the UK and Australia, he was a founding member of The Basement Group (Newcastle-upon-Tyne, 1979-84) and director of the Experimental Art Foundation (Adelaide, Australia, 1991-98). Recent exhibitions of his art work include the solo exhibitions 'Negative Space' (Yuill Crowley Gallery, Sydney, 1999), 'ahistoryofreading' (Kewlona Art Gallery, Canada, 1999) and the group exhibition 'Sporting Life' (Museum of Contemporary Art, Sydney). He has written widely, both as a reviewer and for artists' catalogues.

SUSAN HILLER

Artist Susan Hiller holds the BALTIC Chair in Contemporary Art at the University of Newcastle-upon-Tyne. Her three-screen video installation 'Psi Girls' was recently shown at the Gagosian Gallery in New York (June – July 2001) whilst her large vitrine installation, 'From the

Freud Museum' (1991-96) is currently on show at Tate Modern in London. She is part of the curatorial advisory panel (with Ralph Rugoff and Janos Sugar) for the Biennale of Sydney 2002 and represented Britain this year at the Habana Biennial with her audio-sculpture 'Witness' (2000). This work, originally commissioned by Artangel, was subsequently included in the recent exhibition at Tate Britain, 'Intelligence: New British Art 2000'. Also in 2000, she curated the international, cross-generational group exhibition, 'Dream Machines', which has been shown in Dundee, Sheffield, London and Swansea.

SHARON KIVLAND

Sharon Kivland is an artist, writer and curator who divides her time between the UK and France. She has exhibited widely in Britain, Europe and North America and her recent projects include 'A Case of Hysteria' (1999, Bookworks) and 'Making History', a site-based project organised by Staffordshire University. Since 1997 she has curated seven exhibitions at the Centre for Freudian Analysis and Research, London, and is currently working on a book investigating the psychic relations between the work of art and its viewer. Her most recent work, 'Le Bonheur des Femmes', has been shown at venues in Edinburgh, Quebec City, Montreal and Rennes, and will be followed by a forthcoming catalogue to be published by Editions Filgrane in 2002.

VICKI LEWIS

Vicki Lewis joined BALTIC as curator 1999. Prior to this she worked as an exhibitions organiser at the Hayward Gallery, London, where she was responsible for numerous exhibitions including 'The British Art Show' (1995), 'Howard Hodgkin Paintings' (curated by David Sylvester, 1995), 'Anish Kapoor' (1998) and 'Panamarenko' (curated by Jon Thompson, 2000). She has a Masters Degree in

Visual Arts Administration from the Royal College of Art, London, and co-founded and ran the Diorama Gallery in London from 1985-90. At BALTIC she is responsible, with the director, for developing the programme of exhibitions, commissions, residencies and other events.

PROFESSOR JOHN MILNER

John Milner is Professor of Art History at the University of Newcastle. His numerous publications include studies on the art of the early Soviet period ('Kazmir Malevich and the Art of Geometry', 1996, and 'A Dictionary of Russian and Soviet Artists', 1993) and on late nineteenth-century Paris in 'The Studios of Paris: The Capital of Art in the Late Nineteenth Century' (1988) and most recently, 'Art, War and Revolution: France 1870 – 1871' (2000).

RALPH RUGOFF

Ralph Rugoff is a cultural theorist, writer, curator and the director of the CCAC Institute at the California College of Arts and Crafts in Oakland, California. He has curated a number of exhibitions including 'The Scene of the Crime' (UCLA Hammer Museum, 1997), 'At the Threshold of the Visible: Minuscule and Small Scale Art, 1994-96' (New York Independent Curators), and with Lisa Corrin, 'The Greenhouse Effect' (Serpentine Gallery, London, 2000). He is a regular contributor to Frieze, Artforum, LA Weekly and the Financial Times, and a collection of his essays was published in 'Circus Americanus' (Verso, 1995).

ADAM SZYMCZYK

Adam Szymczyk is a freelance writer and curator based in Warsaw. Since studying on the Curatorial Training Programme at De Appel, Amsterdam, he has curated numerous exhibitions including 'Roundabout' (CCA, Warsaw, 1998) and (with Charles Esche and Mark

Kremer) 'Amateur 1900 and 2000: Variable Research Initiatives' (Kunstmuseum Gothenburg, 2000). Since 1995 he has worked with the Foksal Gallery in Warsaw where he has curated shows of, among others, Susan Hiller, Gregor Schneider and Richard Wright. He has written texts for various art journals and magazines including NU, Metronome and TRANS. He is currently working on the exhibition 'Walk Till the End Of the World', concerned with diverse issues in the writings of Rober Walser and including Francis Alÿs, Franziska Furter, Roman Signer and Piotr Uklanski (December 2001). This will be the first show in the Foksal Gallery Foundation's new space in Warsaw.

ANDY THOMSON

Andy Thomson is an artist and a Lecturer in Painting in the Fine Art Department at the University of Newcastle. Prior to his appointment to the University in 2000, he was Lecturer in Painting at RMIT University in Melbourne, Australia (1989 – 2000). As an artist, he has exhibited at venues in both the UK and Australia including the Centre for Contemporary Photography and ACCA (Australian Centre of Contemporary Art), Melbourne. In 1999 he was Visiting Professor at the Seoul National University and artist-in-residence at the Seocho Institute of Visual Arts, Seoul, Korea. Andy Thomson's current research involves the use of colour, camera obscura, video and other lens-based media that mediate the viewer's perceptual experience of the real.